THE NEW COMMUNITY

THE NEW COMMUNITY

Elizabeth O'Connor

HARPER & ROW, PUBLISHERS

New York Hagerstown San Francisco London

to Mary Jo Cook

FIRST EDITION

LIBRARY OF CONGRESS CATALOG CARD NUMBER: 76–9964

ISBN: 0–06–066337–5

Designed by Dorothy Schmiderer

Contents

Introduction

Through all my books runs the theme of Christian community. I think that there will be no end to my writing of it. The subject is universal and inexhaustible, holding as it does our relationship with each other and our relationship with God. Is this book then for everyone, as the jacket cover would like to say? No, that is hardly true. Many speak and write of Christian community as though it were an easy accomplishment, and imply that the rest of us are overburdened with the matter and should not take ourselves so seriously. "All we have to do is love one another," they say, as though that were something that people are experienced in doing. I doubt that the reader will find in this book encouragement for an easy Christianity. I write for those who are lonely in their hearts, and are searching for what they have not found; for those who ask what Christian community really is, and how they might live it; and for those who may even begin to know, as I begin to know, that what we yearn for and sigh after, we also resist in our inmost selves. This book is for those who have some understanding that genuine community is the highest achievement of humankind, demands more of us than any other endeavor, and is supremely worth the struggle. I have written it out of my own yearnings and search; out of my failings and small victories; in the midst of loneliness and in the midst of community—of alienation and communion.

As always I have drawn upon the stories and experiences of my community of the Church of the Saviour in Washington, D.C., using events in its life almost as parables. They enable me to say in a concrete way what otherwise would remain abstract. If I had been placed in any other community, I would have used its stories and experiences in the same way.

The first chapter concerns the death of a little girl, and illustrates the unity and sense of community that we all touch from time to time. Chapter Two states that we cannot have this kind of community on any sustained basis unless we join in the struggle of the oppressed who are cut off and dying. Jubilee Housing in the third chapter is simply an example of how one segment of my community is attempting to engage in that struggle. The fourth chapter on the Education for a New Society suggests that the transformation of outward structures is dependent on an inner transformation in the lives of those who work for change. Fair warning is given in Chapter Five that any real inward work will in time involve our letting go of forms and structures that now seem safe and permanent. Finally, the last chapter gives a few marks of the new community without intending in any way to describe them fully.

Margaret Williamson Peterson took the photographs of Jennifer used in the first chapter, and Mary Powell the one of the hillside cross. As always the sensitive and thoughtful editing of my friend Dorothy Ham Devers enabled me to give a better work to the publisher. Marie Cantlon, friend and editor at Harper & Row, encouraged and worked with me in all the details of the making of a book. Finally I am warmly grateful for Jean Sensemen, Pat Sitar, Diane Sitar, and Carolyn Tait who typed the manuscript and gave me needed encouragement along the way.

Elizabeth O'Connor

1 Jenny

Hear, you who have ears to hear, what the
Spirit says to the churches! To him who is
victorious I will give some of the hidden
manna; I will give him also a white stone, and
on the stone will be written a new name,
known to none but him that receives it.

Rev. 2:17 NEB

"Behold, how good and how pleasant it is for brethren to dwell together in unity!" (Ps. 133:1 KJV). This scripture is the first line of Dietrich Bonhoeffer's small book, *Life Together,*[1] which grew out of his experience of Christian community in an underground seminary in Nazi Germany. The scripture addresses our real hunger as do the words "life together." And yet anyone who has tried to live in community with others knows how beset with pain and difficulties such a life is! Perhaps that is why the pews in our churches are row on row, and why in less obvious ways we have put distance between ourselves and others. We have not wanted to suffer in any serious way the encountering of one another, all unaware that avoidance deprives us of community that would evoke in our lives the experience of the psalmist.

Oftentimes the further we are from community the deeper is our longing for it. We were created to live in unity with one another. The fruitless search of so many for this genuine experience may be indicative of something more than the lack of true community in the world. What we want and on occasion demand that others give to us, we ourselves do not know how to build, a condition which could be a grave hint of our maldevelopment. Persons thrive and grow and come into full existence in relationship with others, and then themselves become makers of community. But how do we fulfill this divine destiny when we have in our history no meaningful experience of life lived out in depth with others?

While it is true that so many have little experience of "life together," to us all

3

Jennifer Dodge

have come those graceful times when our lives were bound in communion—when knit together by every constituent joint the frame became built up in love. In my own small segment of the Church such a time was the October when Jennifer Dodge, two years and nine months old, did her dying.

For me, though not for Jennifer, it began on a late afternoon when I called her mother to go over a class we were teaching together, and she said, "I am worried about Jenny. She is weaving when she walks. I have made an appointment to take her to see a neurologist next week." That night Jennifer was critically ill and admitted to the children's ward of a Washington hospital. All through the day and night doctors made tests. On Sunday morning they operated to remove a tumor growing on her brain stem. A few hours later she opened her eyes said, "Hi Mommie," then sank into a coma.

A week later the doctors advised another operation, predicting three possible outcomes: one, she would live a normal life for perhaps as long as ten years; two, she would die; and three, she would have to be institutionalized for the rest of her life. The parents made the agonizing decision. The operation was performed. Three days later, the child was dead.

Above the Lake of the Saints, on a rolling hillside of Dayspring, are the woods and open spaces that Jenny had loved to run in, and on, and through. Here we celebrated her life and her death with the planting of the frail tree that she had liked to water when it grew on the back porch of her home. In her arms Joan held her second-born, four-day old Elizabeth. Elizabeth means consecrated to God. Mary Powell read the one-day-old poem that had grown in her.

Fall: are there any fresh words for it?
It is not, as they say, gaudy, except for orange-pink
   maples with black bark;
Rather, the colors are earth colors, intensified.
But it does rush against death—
   a final fling of lightning rods.
The common green of earth flares and flashes up;
Color pushes out through stem and stalk,
   and the leaves dyed bright
   conspicuously, exultantly dying.
And the child I have held two weeks in me,
   the child is dying;
   and the others of us live.
And some inconspicuous love held two years in me
   flashes suddenly,
   and I look at the others here
   carefully and lovingly straight in the eyes.
Then checked by fears of losing all to love or death or both
   for two weeks I clench and unclench my fists;
   and both the loving and the fearing push color up
   my stalks.
Until the child turns loose,
   her bright leaves fall and the branch is bare.
Until I see this dying and embrace my own.
Until yes to Jenny's dying is yes also to loving,
   for both require the same of me.
Then sap rises and red of my own tree comes;
   and, one life gone and one life given,
   my leaves let go of familiar stems.

When the poem had been read, and Jenny's father, her Sunday school teacher and friends had spoken, the father placed the tree in the earth and settled the soil around it. A small boy came forward with an unbalanced cross he had made that morning. On other days when he had nailed pieces of wood together he had called them airplanes, but on this morning he gave his work to his mother saying that it was "a cross for Jenny." It was pushed into the freshly turned ground.

Those gathered on the hillside were held once more in the oneness that in the past week had so many times brought to mind the priestly prayer, "I pray that you may be one even as I am one with the Father." Jenny had always been "a joiner." She perceived our interrelatedness and believed that in the nature of things people were in life together. For a few times I had visited her home with Mary Powell. Thereafter, whenever Jenny and I met, she would ask, "Where is Mary?" When she met Mary, she would inquire, "Where is Betty?" A couple had given her parents a plant, which Jenny always called "the Sue and Peter Plant." We returned to a

"Until I see this dying and embrace my own" (Mary Powell)

child's earlier sayings, a child peering through a banister, a child figuring out mystery.

Her father and mother found deeper places in themselves. They learned not only to care for Jenny in new ways, but to care anew for each other. For this to happen is not as usual as one would think. Only a rare couple goes through an experience like theirs and emerges without serious and often lasting marital difficulties. What probably made the difference was that they were able to share their feelings with each other, and to be honest about those feelings, to turn from offered ways of escape and to save energy for private places in which to scream and to tell it like it was to a God who was not beyond their confrontation. Perhaps this is what enabled them to wait for each other when their timing was not the same, and often it was not. In any relationship there are times when we are not together at the important junctures, and then someone has to wait and the quality of that waiting makes all the difference in the world. Others also waited in the days of Jenny's illness. A team of doctors and nurses postponed for minutes that stretched

A child figuring out mystery

into two hours the second operation while Joan and Doug shared with each other their anguish, hopes, and dread, and finally gave to the waiting surgeon their consent.

The long October of Jenny's dying joined more than her father and mother in deeper bonds. We make so much in our community of the role of spiritual director, and sometimes wonder if any of us is wise enough to be this to another. The church has so elevated the position that today we find ourselves with all too few directors of souls. In those weeks the mortally wounded child became to many of us spiritual director, priest, and prophet, connecting us to that which was deepest in ourselves. In our small mission groups we had said that we were members of one another with unlimited liability for each other, but many of us never really believed that it would prove true—it was not so much our lack of trust in others as lack of trust in our own capacity for responsible love. So often in this community we have gone around testing love—wondering how long it was going to last, when patience would give out or endurance end, always holding back, never believing enough to put our full weight down. In those weeks we discovered that we were indeed members one of the other—that Jenny was child of ours—that our love would last forever, that we were committed to her and her parents in sickness and in health, and wanted the privilege of helping them care for Jennifer, of cherishing and enabling her life, however maimed it might be. When we find love and caring and unlimited liability in ourselves, we no longer need in the same way those qualities in others. When one is tested and found not wanting, one is free to love without asking what the return will be. In those weeks Jenny was the evoker of our richest gifts.

But the fallen child did more than unite us with our deepest selves. She brought us together as a people. Our missions were spread out in twenty different places and we had begun to feel fragmented—to wonder where the unity was that we had known in earlier days when we worked in one place at the same task. Jenny helped us to discover and know again the oneness that had never been far out of reach, but which probably cannot be experienced until our lives are combined in a common struggle. As we waited, prayed together, shared our hopes and our fears, looked once more at our own deaths, and fought for the healing of a child, we moved into a oneness in Christ. With her stripes we were healed.

Is this not what our life is about—a moving toward unity? Had Jenny not accomplished in less than three years what many of us have not done in many more? "I have glorified thee on earth by completing the work which thou gavest me to do." (NEB John 17:4)

Her father said, "Death has always been destructive in my life. It is strange to say it, but in the death of my daughter I have not been diminished. I have experienced the resurrection. I am more alive as a person." And he added, "The quality of your caring had to be rooted in the love of God." What Joan and Doug said of us, we said of them. They let us watch them caring for Jenny, caring for each other, and caring for us. They received us into their presence, shared unashamedly their anguish, let us cry with them and do some of our own unfinished grieving for those whom we had loved and lost in other years. At odd places, at odd times of the day, in long and abbreviated meetings we found ourselves telling our own stories once again, filling in some of the gaps that we had left in other tellings.

The fact that we could relive old sorrows and find strength growing in us is one thing. It is another that the father and mother of Jenny could drink so full a cup of suffering and not be overwhelmed by the pain of it but healed and baptized by the Spirit. This was an important message of those days—that the inevitable result of living deeply into all our feelings is to know the presence of the living God, and to make in one's self discoveries one never thought possible.

The genius of Christianity lies in the fact that it goes to the root of our primal striving by issuing a call to build the Church, and giving to us, in the Old and New Testaments, revolutionary handbooks for the founding of the faith community. The question is, can we consider those books with enough seriousness to be transformed by them, and so follow their instructions for the building of a new society.

The primary purpose of the disciplines, structures of accountability, and mission of the Church is to build life together, to create liberating communities of caring. To each of us is given a gift for the building of a community of caring, a community in which we can learn to embrace our pain, and to overcome all those oppressive inner structures that would keep us in bondage and make us protective and anxious for our own futures.

2 Servant Structures

I dwell in a high and holy place
with him who is broken and humble in
spirit.

Isa. 57:15 NEB

The salient fact about the community we yearn for, and that calls us into wholeness, is that it cannot exist for itself. It exists only in relationship to the world. In recent years we have awakened to the fact that the peoples of this world are largely destitute—without food and clothing and shelter, and without structures that nourish any inward life. Unless a group of persons reach beyond themselves to touch and be touched by some of this need, its members will not know community. This is first of all a spiritual truth, and secondly a well-confirmed psychological truth which is, nonetheless, very difficult to grasp. I occasionally talk to people who are beginning house churches, communes or small study groups, and what they say, in one way or another, is that the mission will have to wait. "Our people have been starved by the churches. They are bone dry and they are hurting. We are going to have to build ourselves up before we can think about mission."

I understand what they are talking about. No one who lives any kind of life in depth with a small group of people can fail to know that each of us has a great deal of suffering to do. Some of that suffering, however, is not real. It comes from work that we were not supposed to do, or did for the wrong reasons. We are replenished by the work that is ours to do and that we do in company with others. This work also injects spirit into the world.

Last week two ministers came to inquire about my community and its life and structures. I responded as best I could in an hour's time. At the end of the discussion they asked, "Are the people here joyful?" I sensed that for them this was the crucial question. If I could answer yes, they would go away convinced that they had found a community that was truly in Christ. A few of the members of my own mission group flashed across my mind: the one who despite his abundant gifts cannot produce even a modest living for his family; another struggling to cope with his wife's depression; one whose marriage was coming to an end; and another whose foster child had run away. But I guess, more than this, the question turned my thoughts to the pain that was deep in me.

I explained to my visitors that we were a community in all different stages, and that some of us were very joyful and that some of us were very sad. When they left I still reflected on the question. Questions like this, and assumptions about the kind of people Christians are, always fill me with self-doubt. Once more I took care of my uneasiness by remembering that the witness of this community is that now and then we manage to transcend our own pain, put aside the unfinished business of our own lives, leave the miry earth which yields under our own feet to be with the stranger in his pain and unfinished business and to stumble with him upon places of healing.

Strangers become friends

In his most extraordinary book, *Pedagogy of the Oppressed,* Paulo Friere calls us to this kind of reaching out when he writes: "We cannot say that in the process of revolution someone liberates someone else, nor yet that someone liberates himself, but rather that men in communion liberate each other."

His words have the poetry of the old prophets. They come on the wind and fall into deep places:

> We flourish in communion with each other. . . . There are no donors or receivers. . . . There are no relationships that are not reciprocal. . . . But freedom isn't something that is given. It is something very arduous, because nobody gives freedom to anyone else, no one frees another, nobody can even free himself all alone; men free themselves only in concert, in communion, collaborating on something wrong that they want to correct. There is an interesting theological parallel to this: no one saves himself all alone, because only in communion can we save ourselves—or not save ourselves.[1]
>
> There is no "I am," nor "I know," nor "I liberate you," nor "I save you"—but rather a "we are," a "we know," a "we liberate one another," and a "we save one another."[2]
>
> As long as I fight, I am moved by hope; and if I fight with hope, then I can wait.[3]
>
> Any delay caused by dialogue—in reality a fictitious delay—means time saved in firmness, in self confidence, and confidence in others, which anti–dialogue cannot offer.[4]

When Bruno Bettelheim commented on the hunger in the world for community, he wrote:

> Today there is a considerable desire for greater communality in living. But the reason most so-called communities usually cannot keep their members and exist on the fringes of society, often as its parasites, lies in a crucial misconception about communal life. Most of these communities are formed "to live the communal life," and therefore concentrate on it. I am convinced communal life can flourish only if it exists for an aim outside itself. Community is viable if it is the outgrowth of a deep involvement in a purpose which is other than, or above that of being a community.[5]

Long before these contemporary prophets, Isaiah was telling us that we grow and thrive only when we reach out to take others into "the family." He cries:

> Enlarge the limits of your home
>   spread wide the curtains of your tent
> Let out its ropes to the full
>   and drive the pegs home (Isa. 54:2 NEB).

This is a scripture to wrap around a wrist as the Vietnamese come to live in our cities and towns and homes—a scripture to help create a friendly space for every

I came upon them unexpectedly and in
those moments my blind eyes were
opened and my deaf ears unsealed;
I saw that beauty is its own excuse
for being

immigrant groaning for hope, and work, and community. Unless words like these find root in us, old myths will come alive. We will think that there is not enough to go around, that we need to protect ourselves, to remember that "they are outsiders who want to know us for what they can take from us," to be suspicious of their motives. We will begin the process of segregation from those with whom we have an opportunity to build international communities, and with whom we can be a sign of the future. "Enlarge the limits of your home" is more than a suggestion. It is the condition of a promise: "Then shall your light break forth like the dawn and soon you will grow healthy like a wound newly healed" (Isa. 58:8 NEB), or "Then, if you call, the Lord will answer; if you cry to him, he will say, 'Here I am' " (Isa. 58:9 NEB).

Much of contemporary writing and preaching describes the mission of the Church in sacrificial terms as though it were something that we do for the sake of others rather than for our own sake. But always the prophets new and old tell us that in giving of ourselves we keep our own lives watered, nor is there any other means of making up for the years when our roots were in parched land and we grew deformed; we had no beauty, no majesty. In our reaching out we rebuild the "ancient ruins" of our own lives, restore all the broken walls that make us feel shaky and insecure.

> The ancient ruins will be restored by your own kindred and you will build once more on ancestral foundations; you shall be called Rebuilder of broken walls, Restorer of houses in ruins (Isa. 58:12 NEB).

In providing a home, we take care of our own homesickness. Each of us prepares her household for the coming of the Lord.

The spiritual law at the core of our being requires that we reach out. We are fulfilled to the extent that we are in relationship. We cannot disobey or even resist this law without suffering. So wondrously are we made that we are happiest when we are loving and miserable when we are not loving. The nature of our own beings witnesses to the nature of God's being. The only task of the church's liberation movement is to free love in others and to free love in ourselves. There is no other way to usher in Christ's "new earth."

The survival of soul, of spirit, of psychic life and personality is dependent on giving and receiving. All relationship must be reciprocal. In one sense no mission to another is possible, since it is through the other that one's own self is realized. I am being killed when there is no one to receive my thoughts, my feelings, my innermost self. Sometimes it happens that we are being killed the whole day long.

Our gifts are not for ourselves alone, or for our own little tribe—the people we know. They are the means by which our energy and personality are released into life—the means of our giving to others what they lack, and of receiving from them what we lack. When we began to consider seriously in our groups the concept that each of us has four functions—sensation, thinking, feeling, and intuition—we drew the conclusion that a person is whole when functioning equally well in all four areas. The goal we set for ourselves and for others was the development of our weaker functions. Now, a number of years later, while this still has an important emphasis in our pilgrimage, we are not as hopeful that any one of us will achieve wholeness in this life. It took a bit of transformation in some of us to accept this attitude and to look to others for what we lacked in ourselves. None of us is complete alone. To recognize that we are complete only in community is to realize that we need not be threatened by the gifts of others. How else, save through their gifts, can others serve us, bear our burdens, give us new thoughts? When I hold the other down, or put him too high up, community is damaged, and gifts are not offered and received.

An inner truth always has a corresponding outer reality. Our interdependence is woven through the fabric of the universe. The painful, fearful, wonderful message of the modern world is that we are members one of the other, and that we cannot live if we are not in communion with each other. This insight which is at the heart of the Gospels is being laid bare in the created order. Ecologists, the present-day prophets of doom, tell us of our interdependence, and declare that there is no healing and sustenance for anyone unless we participate in one another's recovery and growth. One staff member at the United Nations warned that if Brazil continues to cut her timber at the present rate, in time the extensive Amazon forests, source of a significant supply of the world's oxygen, will be substantially reduced, radically affecting the biosphere which supports the life-giving system for everything that breathes. Each week brings new and startling statements. Even when the experts argue and modify them, the fact of our interrelatedness is writ large and clear. The world, even for the hard of learning, is turning out to be one great household—every woman, my sister, every man, my brother.

The city of New York falls into trouble and all American cities tremble the more. The suburbs and rural areas no longer seem independent of the tarnished metropolis. It may even be that the fate of the towns is bound up in the fate of the cities, and that American cities do not exist independently of Sao Paulo, Lagos,

Calcutta, Peking, Bombay, Bangkok, Manila, Lima, and all other exploding, shattered cities of the world: "I will lay your cities in ruin and you shall be made desolate" (Ezek. 35:4 NEB).

Even with all the signs and flash warnings lighting up the skies, it is hard for most of us to believe that our lives are intricately interwoven and that when one falls we all fall. In my own community is the beginning of an awakening to the cruel poverty and injustice in the world, but awareness is far from complete in us. Not yet has it the depth and scope to change radically the way we plan our lives. We know the facts; intellectually we accept them and recite them with conviction to each other, but emotionally they have not penetrated us very deeply. All of our lives we have benefited from many of the structures that have oppressed others. We tend to hold the "wealthy ruling class" responsible for the wrongs we see, and to feel that since the unjust structures of society are not of our making, there is little we can do to change them. We cry out against them, and to ourselves seem caring; to others we seem self-righteous. It is one thing to speak of the need for a more equitable distribution of the world's wealth and resources and another to make

"I will lay your cities in ruin, and you shall be made desolate"
(Ezekiel 35:4 NEB)

available what one has. If the psalms were, indeed, the prayer book of Jesus, how many times did he ponder the words and ask himself the question,

> How can those buried in the earth do him homage,
> How can those who go down to the grave bow before him? (Ps. 22:29 NEB).

Were we asking the same questions when we wondered whether we could serve him better if we became poor, if we put aside our concerns about educating our children, relinquished our hold on careers in order to share the problems and tensions of those who live in our ghettos and the ever deepening agony of the world's poor? Would we find a secret power in poverty—our true vocation in a larger struggle?

While the questions plagued us, we continued to be too much a part of our culture to consider seriously any radical move in another direction. We liked the clear picture on TV, and preferred it to be in color. We had air conditioning in our houses, and aspired to have it in our cars. We took our vacations in far places and bought unessential items in the market places. We frequented our favorite restaurants, enjoyed the gourmet food, and reasoned that we were making our contribution to the functioning of the economy. In one way or another we asked ourselves:

> How could we buried in the ghetto do him homage?
> How could we cast away in tenements bow before him?

Time and time again the discussions, put to rest, would be revived when one of us would have our imagination captured by a person or a community: Mother Teresa, moving among the dying of India; Tulio Vinay fighting for the workers of Sicily; Dorothy Day feeding New York's hungry; or Koinonia Farms struggling to make it possible for some of the South's poor to own homes. Someone would say, "There is a life that I would like to touch"; and someone else would answer, "But the situation is different with us. We are not a community that pools its wealth and has economic responsibility for its members. Who will care for us when we are sick or old, and besides, there are other calls than the call to the poor. If that happens to be your call, why don't you answer it, and let me answer mine?" Sometimes the words were angry and the tone accusing. We often concluded that nothing more was required of us. Somehow the world would get itself together, and all the crumbling systems would begin to serve us once again. Then came the newspapers with the wide and empty eyes of starving children looking out from the pages, and once more members of our company would return to the question of how to position ourselves with the wretched of the earth, and how to deal with our own fears of not having enough—of becoming needy in a world that holds the poor in such large contempt. We did not often feel certain that bread cast upon the waters comes back unless all cast their bread. We wanted assurance of the company of one another in so hazardous an undertaking as alliance with the oppressed. And yet we knew that if each waited for the other no one would move. "Here am I. Send me," is a lonely declaration, but it signals a life at one with itself.

In recent years the conflict has deepened in many of us. Inner wars go on. We recite the promises of the gospel, but the fact is that we do not believe them wholeheartedly. We want to help with the overwhelming needs of the poor, but a part of us wonders how we will take care of our own overwhelming needs. We hate all the sermons about the oppressed "out there," when we have all those poor "in here," and yet we faintly know that the destinies of those two groups are intertwined.

So many times I find myself caught in an inner revolution. An old existing order is threatened by a new one. When I step aside and watch I usually want the new to win, but some days it looks as though all the old people will stay in power. On other days it looks the other way—as if all the old will be swept away and replaced by the new. On occasion it becomes an absorbing battle that takes all my time and energy. In small spaces I work, and eat, and think about God, but everything is for the sake of the revolution.

We have been innocent if we have not known that conflict is a large component in change. The greater the change, the deeper the conflict. The old in us argues and fights to maintain things as they are, clinging to that which is known and secure and promises protection. We cannot overcome our dependencies and fear, and acquire a whole new liberating attitude, and at the same time keep everything as it is. If something new comes into being in us—if *metanoia* happens, something old has had to make way for it. This is how conflict is resolved. Old positions are given up and one's life becomes unified around the new, which then becomes the place of God's rest; but camp will have to be broken again for we are the people of the Exodus, the people who have a pilgrim feast to keep. "Birds of the air have nests; but the Son of man has nowhere to lay his head" (Luke 9:58 RSV). The long trek out of bondage is not over. The liberation movement progresses to a new stage in its history. Other conflicts will have to be fought and won, but each time we have more inner territory upon which to stand. We know better that we did not create the revolution. It is God's revolution. He is the one who abhors all forms of oppression, and will complete the work he has begun.

Several years ago I heard a theologian say that the book of Exodus was the most important book for our time. Since then I have kept these Scriptures close at hand, and many times have turned to ponder them and find courage and instruction for the revolution in me and the revolutions in the world, discovering for myself why Moses, our Christ of the Old Testament, towers so large a figure, a model for all revolutionaries. It is easy to identify with the beginnings of this first revolutionary, for surely conflict raged in him. Was he to cast his lot with the rich or the poor? He had been raised in an affluent household with the education and privileges that wealth bestows. His foster mother was a stately, tender, and most likely beautiful woman, but there probably came a day when she thought him old enough to be told that he was not of royal lineage, but a member of the hated Hebrew race. "You are not Egyptian, but Hebrew in a land where Hebrew is not beautiful." Or was it an adored and adoring slave woman who drew him aside to whisper, "I am your real mother"? Whatever else went on in the young Moses we know that anger raged in him. Perhaps his slow speech had obscured from others the brilliance of his mind and caused the court to compare him unfavorably with the Pharaoh's sons. Or was the halting speech itself the result of a child's inability to handle unequal treatment? Whatever the case, Moses had injustices of his own for which to seek redress, and conflicting claims upon him when he went out to his kinsmen and saw them at their heavy labor.

The Hebrews do not accept Moses as one of them. Suspicion and distrust are not easily overcome. At best they view him as a "do-gooder." *Even* the one he befriends joins with his opponent against the "outsider": "Who set you up as an officer and judge over us?" These words echo in the New Testament when Jesus refuses to play the role that Moses so quickly assumed. When asked to settle an argument Jesus replies, "My good man, who set me over you to judge or arbitrate?" (Luke 12:13 NEB).

When Moses returns from his long exile he is not only the son confronting the father, but the enemy of an oppressive power structure. Is not our task the same: to confront the fathers who brought us up with too narrow a concept of family and of nation; to let them know that we want to claim our membership in another household, that the earth and all that is in it belong to everyone, that nothing in the world comes before a human person, that every man and woman and child is kin of ours? If some of us have more than others, perhaps the dark reason is that we have taken more, or have held back more than is our share.

Greed in the world today is the greatest contradiction of our interdependence and of the understanding of ourselves as a global community. Kosuko Koyama of Asia has named it as "the unclean spirit number one." I say "ah, yes", to this

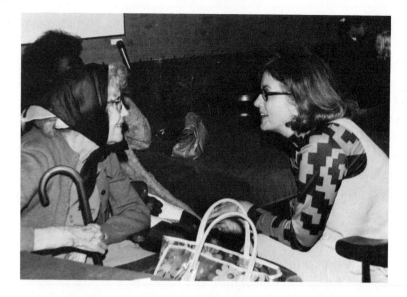

The liberation movement progresses to
a new stage in its history

The ones who gather together to break
their bread

common observation, but not because the world is sunk in greed and destroying itself, but because sometimes I am able to watch myself in the act of taking more, and it has made me afraid. I do not want to be robbed of the revolutionary vocation that I have as a Christian, and I am quite confident that this is what greed does to us. In the end it leaves everyone poor. I give more attention these days to what the saints say about "self-denial," as well as more attention to what modern psychology says about the "realization of potential." These two concepts are better fellow workers than we have thought. There is no realization of self-potential without community, and no community without self-denial.

Greed in us is difficult to understand, but since every human being comes equipped with such a large capacity for it, we can be quite confident that we need to search it out in ourselves. Perhaps by the peculiar quality of its emptiness it can help turn us to another way. Our greed for things, for experience, for diversion and pleasure may be the loss of touch with the inner world and its storehouse of treasures. So much of what we take adds to the craving for more. No hunger in us is satisfied. The gnawing remains, and may simply be the symptom of a deeper ache. Of one thing we can be sure, greed will go away only when we take time to confront it and hear its message, inquire where it is taking us, and ask ourselves if that is where we really want to go. It will not go away if we keep it covered, nor will it go away if we use it as an accusation to stone ourselves or to stone others. That only makes us all the poorer inwardly and adds to greed in the world.

When I am injured, lose my friend, feel overlooked, or that my work does not count for anything, I begin to reach for things as though they had the power to give comfort or protection. I feel at the mercy of ill winds, apprehensive about the future, concerned about what will become of me. Old dreads come back. When someone gets through with the message that I am valued and needed, and have a place in the scheme of things, I stop my clutching of myself to myself. Only then are my fears turned back.

Our primary task is somehow to find a way to say to each other and to the greedy of the world, "You are needed," and to mean it when we say it, because if we do not mean it, it will not count. Che Guevara said, "At the risk of seeming ridiculous let me say that a true revolutionary must be guided by great feelings of love." Paulo Friere calls himself an "apostle of the obvious." I am reminded of these statements because I, too, feel absurd to be writing about things that everyone knows. But perhaps something more makes us all "vagabonds of the obvious." We know that we do not fully understand or live out the commonplace truths that we speak to one another. Our lives are full of conflict. We want to do right, but "only the wrong is within reach" (Rom. 7:21 NEB).

It is the great insight of the modern age that we are beginning to understand that the contradictions in us arise out of our failure to educate our feelings, to know that they are worthy of our attention, and that we can trust them to tell us what has real value and what is counterfeit and a poor substitute for what we really need and want. Perhaps the land of Canaan toward which we journey is a land in which people learn to care about feelings, and learn to educate their feelings.

The gift of knowing is absolutely essential, but it is not complete in itself. We must know that one-fifth of the people of the world are hungry, but we must also begin to feel with the hungry. It is simply not enough to be aware of the injustices of society. The contrast between what we have and what others have may stir conflict in us, but it will not be easily resolved. If we are to do anything about injustices, we must feel them, and face the fact that it is painful to feel. We cannot keep protecting ourselves from sights and smells and sounds that are disturbing. We are not going to become truly radicalized until we get close enough to the oppressed to hear their groans and see their plight. "He heard their groaning, and remembered this covenant with Abraham, Isaac and Jacob; he saw the plight of Israel, and he took heed of it" (Exod. 2:24 NEB). It is not enough to expose our minds to literature about the third world. We have to expose our hearts also, which means that we will have to look, and hear, and touch, and smell: "now the ears of my ears awake and now the eyes of my eyes are opened."

I have sometimes thought that if I could walk among the hungry of Bangladesh or of India, there would be a healing of the division within me, and I could find a lifestyle more consistent with the message of the Gospels. Now I know this is an unreal fantasy. Every nation has its own third world living within its borders. Probably every city and county in America has its powerless and vulnerable hidden away from what we like to think is our sensitive glance. The people I know who have made any radical shift in the way they live have had some exposure to poverty on a consistent basis. When the crossing is made from the world of the elite to that vast world of the poor, they cease to see their work as sacrificial. They begin to care about different things, to acquire a whole new set of values. They are doing what they most want to do. Life has meaning because they feel themselves to be engaged in the important struggles, and along the way they win a friend here and there who is in the same struggle, and soon they have a community.

The real problem with the structures of the Church is that they do not often allow us to become engaged in the anguish of people whose needs, and accents, and ways are different from our own. They do not allow us to feel. It was not enough for

Moses to see the misery of a slave people. He had to identify with them—to be able to say, "My people."

Our quest for community will not end until we come upon the ones who gather together to break their bread with the stranger. There is no other way to have a communion supper. "Look, I am standing at the door, knocking. If one of you hears me calling and opens the door, I will come in to share his meal, side by side with him" (Rev. 3:20 JB).

3 The People of Jubilee

I have called you by name and you are my
own.
When you pass through deep waters, I am
with you,
    when you pass through rivers,
    they will not sweep you away;
walk through fire and you will not be
    scorched,
through flames and they will not burn you.
For I am the Lord your God,
    the Holy One of Israel, your deliverer.

Isa. 43:2–3 NEB

A coffeehouse on a street in the inner city has been the scene of so much of our history. More than that, it has had a peculiar place in the development of many of our lives and thus of our growth and direction as a community. In the past years it has given to us an acquaintance with the city and an exposure to its life that we did not foresee and never would have chosen, but now would find hard to give up. All of which underscores the conviction that part of the education of a people is opportunity for new involvements.

Fourteen years ago when we were looking for suitable quarters, most of us wanted the coffeehouse to be in the fashionable Georgetown area of Washington, and felt frustrated and discouraged when we could not find rental space there. None of us had the poor in mind when we were thinking of a coffeehouse. We even called it our ministry to the "up and out." We settled for the empty store on Columbia Road because in ten months of looking, we had found nothing else, and it did have the advantage of being within ten minutes of our headquarters building on the much more respectable Massachusetts Avenue, known in the city as "embassy row."

The ghetto streets behind the Potter's House were hidden from our sight and none of us gave them much attention. Across the street were some fairly nice apartment houses where people of middle income lived, and this gave us encouragement. Over the years the houses and streets have deteriorated so slowly that going into the neighborhood now causes us no cultural shock, though a great number of us live on safer, cleaner city streets, or in suburbia.

After the riots of 1968 most middle-class whites and blacks avoided the Columbia Road area, feeling that it was too dangerous. Many are still apprehensive, and vast numbers who live in the suburbs do not come into the city at all. For those who have staffed the Potter's House over the years the city does not have that ominous climate—perhaps because we call it home, we do not people its dark streets with the same menacing outlines that one encounters on streets that are unfamiliar. All through the years the Potter's House has been open in the evenings until midnight, so that it is usually one o'clock before the last folk leave. There was a time when the police would stop by to escort us to our cars, but they have long since left us to keep each other company in that morning hour when even our road has a hushed presence. In the past two years we "enlarged the limits" of our home to include the blocks behind the Potter's House, an area which has also lost much of its threat. We now have to remind each other to be cautious, and not to leave anything of value in our parked cars.

The journey from the first days of the coffeehouse to the present time with a whole new movement underway has been a long one. Some of us have borne it all with a debonaire spirit; others, perhaps because of temperament, or because we had so much to learn, or as we liked to think, "had more sense," tossed and turned on our beds and thought it all out through scores of sleepless nights. For many of our number, as for many throughout the nation, the experience of Selma was an important stage of the journeying that gave to us new understandings of oppression which were to change our emphases and direction as a people. The war in Vietnam was to further a process already begun. Being situated in the capital we were from the beginning exposed to many contradictory opinions on the war. At the outset we became involved with the Committee of Responsibility, established to give medical aid to wounded Vietnamese children, a cause with which we were happy to be allied because it took no political stand on the war. The more we listened, however, and worked for the children, the sharper the issues became for our community. Many of us deserted early positions of neutrality and began to seek ways to register protest, but our only real involvement was in response to the leadership of those who organized the peace demonstrations. We would make our colorful banners the night before a peace rally, gather next morning on the church lawn, and begin the three-mile walk to the Washington Mall, joined by others along the way until our numbers swelled to thousands upon thousands.

We often argued among ourselves the effectiveness of those marches of protest and conscience, for the people in power seemed so little affected by them. Over the months we began to see them as the only prophetic word any of us was speaking.

They were in themselves a call to repentance. Whether they were successful or not became unimportant. The marchers by their presence were proclaiming another way, witnessing to the fact that America was not united in war. But for some the marches were much more personal. They were an individual word, the word we had to speak for our own sake in order to keep from falling into apathy and despair —even more important, to keep the fire in our own bones burning. That seems essential now. So often we do nothing, because what there is to do does not seem worth the doing, or is apt to be proved wasted effort, or because we feel that there is something bigger to be done, if we only knew what it was.

The marches helped to preserve soul in us and to create our lives as any action does. We came to hate most of the news coverage of the peace demonstrations because cameras and pens seemed always poised to record the harsh words or the threatening gestures that were so rare in those crowds of 50,000. None of our group ever witnessed an unruly or even mildly unpleasant person. Reporters and TV cameras made no effort to communicate to America the spirit and beauty of peaceful, colorful, singing people—young, middle-aged, old, black, yellow, white— the dividing walls of partition broken down, sharing their lunches, and sharing a day of hope and prayer.

The marches helped to root us in new levels of being. There was the time when some of us deserted our own company to walk with the veterans who were in wheel chairs as well as on foot. A peace came to me on that day and a feeling of solidarity with the poor that I have always wanted and very few times realized in my own life, so that I still struggle for a more concrete involvement in the struggle of the oppressed.

Perhaps that was yet another reason why many of us were in the marches. We had to know what to do next. What shall I do? What can we do? Answers are given when questions are asked with the totality of one's being, and the marches were the closest we could come to putting our minds and hearts and bodies into the question.

After those days we positioned ourselves more strongly as a community on the side of nonviolence, outruling war as a possible solution to any of the world's problems, and rewriting a line of our member's commitment to read:

> Realizing that Jesus taught and exemplified a life of love, I will seek to be loving in all relations with other individuals, groups, classes, races, and nations and will seek to be a reconciler, living in a manner which will end all war, personal and public.

It is always easier to march for peace than to try to create peace in one's own life, or peace between one's life and other lives. After the demonstrations and the poor people's marches, the newspapers began to give more and more space to the worsening housing crisis in the city and to the people who were suffering so silently, growing poorer and poorer while they struggled to pay slum landlords exorbitant rents for wretched apartments with rusted-out plumbing, falling plaster, and scurrying rats. No up-to-date statistics existed on abandoned or substandard houses and apartment buildings but, according to one District government official, if housing codes for condemnation were enforced, 50,000 people would have to be displaced. The shortage of low-income housing had become so great that, for the first time in the history of the capital, thousands of people who were unable to pay rents asked by landlords had become "squatters," breaking into abandoned buildings and living there rent free.

We began to see with different eyes the boarded up apartment building a few doors from the Potter's House, the ghetto of the back streets, and all the decaying firetrap apartments and row houses where the poor lived in crowded miserable rooms, existing in what one reporter called "Dickensian squalor." Could we be against violence and not against all the covert structures of violence that grind to pieces the lives of people?

Adding to our enlightenment were *The Prison Meditations of Father Delp* in which he wrote:

> An "existence minimum" consisting of sufficient living space, stable law and order and adequate nourishment, is indispensable. The "socialism of the minimum" is not the last word on the subject but the essential first word, the start. No faith, no education, no government, no science, no art, no wisdom will help mankind if the unfailing certainty of the minimum is lacking.[1]

As we came to see more clearly the faces of those submerged in the crushing poverty of our own city, it became obvious that only those engaged in the struggles of the poor were going to be able to speak to them any message of God's reign. At the Potter's House the conversation turned once again to what we might do. Each of the groups was struggling anew to define its mission. Those who staffed the Potter's House on Thursday night turned their thoughts to the massive problem of housing in the District. It seemed to them that the best way to eradicate the creeping blight and decay of the city was to purchase housing in the area, to work with the tenants to upgrade it without raising rents, and then to begin a program of education, literacy, recreation, and counseling that would engender hope and spread to the larger community. The more they talked the larger grew the vision of all the people of the city engaged in the transformation of the city.

Though the members of the Thursday night group half guessed that this would mean some sharing of the wealth—a basic Old and New Testament teaching—they had very little idea then, nor have they now, of how this might affect any of our community, or whether we were ready for it in any significant way. The new mission, nonetheless, took the name of Jubilee Housing, after the Jubilee Year in the Old Testament which was established to "proclaim liberty throughout the land to all its inhabitants" (Lev. 25:10 RSV).

In the Jubilee Year, which was the fiftieth year in a cycle of fifty, all debts were to be canceled, land returned to former owners, and any Jew, who for one reason or another had become enslaved to a fellow Jew, was to be set free. That year was established by the early community of God's people as a year of reflection in which to recall their own deliverance from bondage, and their responsibility before God to be a community of justice, and caring, and freedom. Moses again and again

The more they talked the larger grew the vision

instructed his community that in the new land that God was giving to them no person was to be in need:

> Is there a poor man among you, one of your brothers, in any town of yours in the land that Yahweh your God is giving you? Do not harden your heart or close your hand against that poor brother of yours, but be open-handed with him and lend him enough for his needs (Deut. 15:7–8 JB).

Moses took into account the weaknesses of human nature when he added:

> Do not allow this mean thought in your heart, '. . . the year of the remission is near,' and look coldly on your poor brother and give him nothing . . . Of course there will never cease to be poor in the land; I command you therefore: Always be open-handed with your brother, and with anyone in your country who is in need and poor (Deut. 15:9–11 JB).

Because of the unprecedented events that were to take place in the Jubilee Year, it was occasionally referred to as the Year of Liberty, or the acceptable year of the Lord, sometimes translated as the year of the Lord's favor. It was the Jubilee Year that Jesus used to define his own ministry when he stood in the synagogue and read from Isaiah:

> The spirit of the Lord is upon me
>   because he has anointed me;
> he has sent me to announce good news to the poor,
>   to proclaim release for prisoners
>   and recovery of sight for the blind;
> to let the broken victims go free,
> to proclaim the year of the Lord's favour
>
> (Luke 4:18–19 NEB).

The members of Jubilee Housing had no less a mission in mind than to put an end to poverty in the city, to secure decent housing for every person at a cost that each could afford, "to proclaim the year of the Lord's favor." As a beginning, a young member of the group secured a real-estate license and began to investigate the deteriorating structures in the streets behind the Potter's House. She finally managed to track down the absentee owner of two apartment houses that seemed in desperate need of attention. They turned out to belong to a wealthy octogenarian living alone in a hotel room. He was much too shrewd to reveal how eager he was to be rid of the buildings, and Carolyn was much too shrewd to reveal that the group on whose behalf she was negotiating had no money. One apartment house was called the Ritz and the other the Mozart, which made everyone laugh, but an old-time tenant explained that once the decrepit buildings had been well represented by their names. This tenant even remembered the red carpets and high-backed chairs that had been in the lobby of the Ritz.

While the Ritz and the Mozart were in better condition than most ghetto dwellings, both were in an advanced stage of deterioration—roofs that no longer kept the rain out, plumbing that didn't work, no adequate locks on the doors, steel mailboxes twisted open, urine-drenched halls, chewing gum and graffiti on the walls, garbage piled two floors high in the stairwells, and overrun with rats and roaches—everything that one finds in slum buildings.

In times between waiting on tables at the Potter's House, members of Jubilee made plans for the two buildings. One night they shared their wild ideas with an old friend who dropped by for coffee. He, a mortgage banker who had worked all his life with real estate, had some wild dreams of his own for the renewal of cities. More than this, he was grasped by a crazy gospel message that God's liberation movement had to do with human victims trapped in the squalid, plundered dwellings of the world's cities. It was easy for him to fall in with the spirit of the group and to offer to arrange the loan for the down payment on the Ritz and the Mozart. On the first of November 1973, the two apartment buildings became the property of Jubilee Housing, Incorporated. Two days later the District of Columbia

Gordon Cosby is advised by professionals on the renovation of apartments

served the new owners with a three-page list of 900 violations of the housing code.

Gordon Cosby asked his congregation to devote some of the time usually given to preparing for Christmas to help with the renovation of the apartments. All kinds of people responded—young and old, skilled and unskilled labor. The more hardy souls were put to work scrubbing the halls and shoveling out garbage. Others were assigned to painting, carpentry, and plastering. One of our members who owned a paint and wallpaper store donated hundreds of rolls of wallpaper, and a store was set up in the basement so that tenants might come in and select the wallpapers they wanted. A congressional assistant was appointed to assist with this activity, while an electrical engineer who was accustomed to spending his free time on golf courses was assigned to supervise the task of replacing defective light fixtures. There was a place for everyone's gift to be used. Those who were not able to come sent money and supplies. One man was so carried away by the spirit of good will that he reached into a storehouse not his own, and explained unashamedly that the items he was handing out had been appropriated from the military base where he was stationed. Ethical problems like that arose and work had to stop while they were dealt with, but it seemed likely that a carpenter teacher had taught his own class in ethics as he went about his work of ministry.

People who never in a million years would have seen the inside of a slum apartment were engaged in the renovation of one. Workshops in paperhanging, glass cutting, and plastering were scheduled. Janet Colwell, an assistant at CBS, was given the job of scavenging for paints and materials. Chief Charwoman, she called herself. Terry Flood, mother of four, whose experience was the efficient running of her own household, became the manager of both the Ritz and the Mozart. Each day families appeared in her office asking to be put on waiting lists for apartments. Some were pleading, holding babies in their arms and crumpled bills in their hands, reminiscent of another Christmas and another family.

To some of us it seemed that we had stumbled on the appropriate way to celebrate the Christmas season. We gave each other gifts of paint rollers, overalls, and books with useful titles, like *The Boiler Room: Questions and Answers,* and took our children to the lighting of the Christmas tree in the lobby of the Ritz. By the time Christmas came again, word of the enterprise had reached the Vale Technical Institute which runs an automotive trade school outside Pittsburgh, Pennsylvania. The students responded by locating a forsaken bus and using their skills to restore its engine and interior. They then gave it a sleek yellow finish, printed *Jubilee Community* on both sides, and delivered it to the children of the Ritz and the Mozart with a Santa Claus at the wheel.

There was a place for everyone's gift

Christmas hope arrives through a donated bus

The Ritz had sixty apartments and the Mozart had thirty. Most of them had one or two bedrooms; a few had three. The families could not be transferred to other apartments while we worked in theirs, so we had to ask them whether they would help us, their landlords, renovate their apartments while they continued to live in them. Since the only alternative was to try to find quarters in the city that might be even worse, they of course said yes.

The people of Jubilee had much to learn in those early days. As best we knew ourselves, we wanted to give up our elitist positions, but none of us knew fully what that meant, or how to do it. Meetings were called, and a tenant on each floor was elected to serve on a council of moderators. At first the response was enthusiastic, but before long participation began to fall off. Part of the difficulty grew out of the

Gordon Cosby and Crystal Venable, an apprentice

The finishing touch

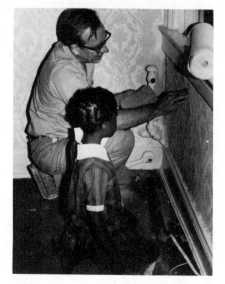

Work well done

fact that Jubilee had not fully worked out its own identity. Some of the members saw themselves as landlords who were obliged to provide attractive and livable quarters for the residents. Others saw themselves as part of a liberation movement whose true leaders had to emerge from the masses trapped in all the squalid hovels of the world.

Each of these concepts was equally valid and needed to exist with the other. The housing code violations had to be corrected and the payments on the buildings had to be made for neither the District Housing agency nor the banking institutions were going to wait while the tenants, together with Jubilee, hammered out a new vision and mode of existence. During the following two years structures enabling the tenants a larger participation in the decision-making and eventually in the ownership of the buildings evolved slowly, and not without arguments, tears, and repentance.

As we worked in the apartments we came to know the tenants—to call each other by name, and sometimes to share our stories. In the telling of their stories we heard what our brothers and our sisters had against us. Jesus said, "If, when you are bringing your gift to the altar, you suddenly remember that your brother has a grievance against you, leave your gift where it is before the altar. First go and make your peace with your brother, and only then come back and offer your gift" (Matt. 5:23–24 NEB). We listen still to the hostility and pain of those who have grievances against us, and who identify us as their oppressors and the perpetrators of the structures that oppress them.

But something else has happened so visible and loud that you can see and hear and feel it when you open the doors of those apartment houses—a community has been called into being; a congregation has been born. It happened in spite of the fact that our work crews were free to work only at night and on weekends, disturbing households for weeks on end. While this gave us opportunity to be in relationship with persons living in the apartments, it also put considerable strain on those relationships. Our clumsiness did not make things easier. There was the paint that was spilled in the middle of the living room rug, and the ceiling that fell while we stood back to admire it. Under the stress of these situations we all said things that had been on our minds right along, and some of us threw in some ancient grievances as well. Fortunately these times were balanced out by other occasions.

The meetings of the Jubilee mission became a new version of the revival meeting, where each gave small testimonials to moments of grace. At one meeting Mary Powell, who had worked for a whole week in a vacant apartment got up and said:

I liked most the contact with the people. Two mornings this week there were two women who came from upstairs. They just walked in and asked, "Have you got anything to do?" So I pointed out the various jobs. They came for two days and talked a lot about who they were and who I was and they said, "This is better than watching TV all day." Yesterday the little girl who is going to live in this apartment came down. She was a fifth grader and really cute. . . . Her room was going to be painted yellow and she and I sat down together and I asked her the kind of yellow she wanted in her room and then we mixed the paints until it got to be just the color she wanted, and then we put it on the wall together.

The human contacts hold the greatest appeal for most of us. Sammie Jones, who, with a friend, had taken on a whole apartment, followed Mary Powell's testimonial with one of her own.

The other day the man across the hall from where we were working was locked out. He was in his robe and pajamas and he stayed outside his door the whole day. He was content with the fact that he would not be able to get in until late in the day when someone else would come home with a key. He walked in and out to talk to us. He was hungry and he said, "Will you get me something to eat?" So we went and got a fishburger for him at MacDonalds. I came back really tired, trudging up the steps, and I rounded the corner and he said, "You come back?" and I said, "Sure," and he said, "Man, I didn't think you would come back," and I sat down in the hall with him and a little bare-bottomed girl that was romping back and forth and we just shared our lives. He told me about where he had been, and how he felt about life, and I thought, this would never have happened in any other way. I am here and I am so glad for it. A few days later, after I had walked up four flights for about the sixth time, Mrs. S. said, "When are you going to rest, girl?" And I said, "I don't know." And she said, "Come on in and I will give you some beef stew." So we sat down to delicious beef stew in her apartment. We were giving to each other. It was miracle to me because I had never expected that this would happen. I had expected to feel good about doing something else for someone, but I did not expect to make friends and have people do things for me.

Statistical reports on rent collections and delinquencies, as well as fund-raising possibilities, were presented at these meetings, but it was obvious that even these concerns had to do with the building of a community that would make it easier for people to love one another. In 1972, soon after the buildings had been acquired, a commercial engineering firm had stated that $192,500 would be required to effect the renovation. In April of 1975, fifty of the ninety units, the lobby areas and some basement rooms had been rehabilitated, the elevator overhauled, and a heating

"This place is too narrow; make room
for me to live in" (Isaiah 49:20 NEB)

plant replaced in the Ritz. The work had been accomplished with 25,000 hours of volunteer labor, at the substantially lower figure of $165,000. That amount of volunteer labor caused the insurance people considerable difficulty. They simply could not comprehend what was going on. Before their disbelief turned to belief their letters carried paragraphs of obvious irritation:

> When the application was submitted to the Bureau there was indication that there are twenty-five volunteer employees. And, in view of this, we feel that we would appreciate your having the insured provide us with a photocopy of the log that they have kept up until now. We hardly see it is possible that the carpenters, paperhangers, electricians and painters would volunteer their help gratis and in view of this we must ask your immediate cooperation in getting this information to us.

In the early days when the movement was new and before it had been claimed by the poor as their own movement, Jubilee members, at a forum on housing, were questioned concerning paternalism: "How do you avoid being labeled paternalistic? Isn't it likely to be said of you, 'Here comes whitey from the suburbs with all the answers on how we should run our lives!' "?

A member of a Jubilee task force replied, "That's a question we ask ourselves every week when we go down there. For instance, we began fixing up an apartment to meet the housing code requirements. That was all we planned to do, but we have encountered other problems. The apartment, partially destroyed by fire, is occupied by a fluctuating number of people. The head of the household, an admirable, hard-working woman, has no supervision for her children. Among other things we discovered she had practically no dishes, and she is behind in her rent. How to respond to those needs without being paternalistic? Do we go up and say, 'Here is some money—your problems are solved'? We have learned to get into the middle of the problem and to see it not as a problem that we solve, but one that we share in. It is a matter of perception. We have to be sure that we are not viewing the people as somehow inferior to ourselves. Their problems are the same as ours—for we all share in the human condition. We come up with acceptable solutions not because we are better or know better, but because we have worked them out together with those who are more involved than we."

Another person added:

I don't know which comes across with more negativity—racism or paternalism. I have heard both sides. I think they are equally unwelcomed. Paternalism is more to be feared perhaps because it is more insidious. Racism is easier to identify. Usually the people who express it know themselves. But paternalism is masked from ourselves and for that reason it is one of the biggest problems we encounter. Reflection is essential. We have to take time to stop and ask, "What is really going on here? What are the reactions, the vibrations?" so that we are not bulldozing through, assuming that our objective is the right objective. We have to wait until we sense that what we are doing is in some way of the Spirit. I believe this happens when we stay on speaking terms with the oppressed in ourselves, and know that we labor for our own liberation, and that we labor on behalf of each other, and on behalf of a city that we want to make work for every one.

Fred Taylor, who has for many years pleaded the cause of abandoned children, injected another note:

You have to remember that some of us grew up in a time when stronger folk told weaker folk what to do—older folk told younger folk. Kathryn Campbell came out of that tradition. We watched the way she worked and a lot of us called it "maternalistic," but the fact is that good things happened for children because of her. If people are going to grow, they have to come to the place of rebelling against that kind of assistance, but without her a lot of people would never have come to the place of rebelling at all, or of even existing in any important way.

Gordon Cosby answered the question in still other words:

The spirit in which we go must be a spirit rooted in Christ—in his life and power. The ultimate victory will be achieved in him when all things are united, and we all have learned what we needed to learn. The other side of paternalism is worse than paternalism, and that is that we become so fearful of controlling others or of creating dependence that we do nothing. We begin to feel that we have no answers, and that we have nothing to give, and fade out of the picture altogether, critical of the efforts of others who are willing to take risks and make mistakes in a struggle to find a way out for those trapped in a morass of poverty.

Part of Jubilee's effort to find a way out was the initiation of wide support programs based on tenant participation. One of the mini-institutions that sprang up was the Jubilee Freedom Institute. The Institute was organized as a "free university," which meant that anyone within the apartment community could propose a course that he or she would like to take, or teach, or coordinate. If there was sufficient response the proposed course became part of the curriculum. Whenever possible, courses were organized and offered by teaching teams composed of both tenants and members of the church community. The school began with thirty-five students and five classes: Reading Improvement, Introduction to Office Skills, Creative Photography and Darkroom Technique, Understanding the Bible, Making Your Own Clothes. I am in the photography class. We have had six classes taught by a member of the Church's Creativity Group. Recently we became excited about the work we were doing. One man said, "I would like to photograph the city at night," and then added thoughtfully, "It is one beautiful city at night." Another said, "I just want to photograph its buildings—all its different kinds of buildings." We hope we can do these things. Together we may even discover the meaning of the city, entering into an I-Thou relationship with its buildings, its streets, and, of course, its people through the medium of a camera rather than with the help of a guru. This is how one becomes a contemplative—discovering that at the center of the city's life is love, and coming to understand that the pain which is there helps us to know that we are out of touch with this love.

Every class in the Jubilee Freedom School has its own story. The typing class meets in the offices of a local broadcasting company at the invitation of a company executive, who six months ago would not have dreamed of committing himself to such folly. The employees of a branch of Xerox are considering ways of becoming involved. As other people in other places hear what is happening they are beginning to come to work in the apartments. The wives of congressmen came for a Saturday, others for a weekend or a year. The doctors in our own congregation joined with the young medical students of our city's black university to give each person in the Ritz and the Mozart a complete physical examination.

In the meantime the unused and dilapidated basement rooms were turned into a coffeehouse for the tenants and a meeting room for the elderly. The room where the neighborhood had once received its heroin shots and conducted its other traffic in drugs became the classroom of a Montessori school. We began to dream of a time

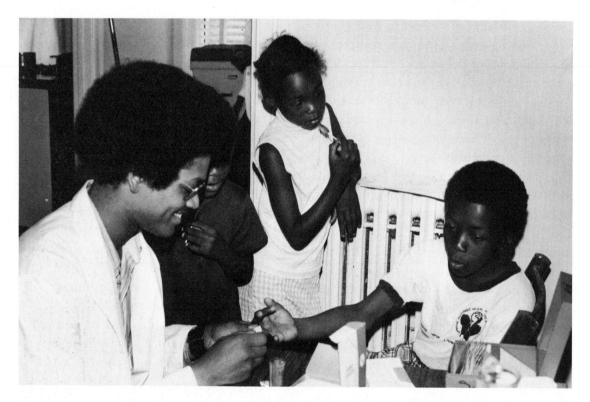

A renovated apartment becomes a health clinic

"The child learns his lowliness or his self-assurance near the fireplace and in front of the grocer or druggist"
(Robert Coles)

when the city's unused real-estate and basement areas would be turned into mini-recreational and educational institutions to nourish the community and tend the life of the young.

If adults were sometimes suspicious and slow to respond, their fears and prejudices were not passed on to their children. The children of the Ritz and the Mozart were always on hand, some shy and silent, listening to thoughts of their own; others were full of energy, questions, and oftentimes, a kind of frenzy. From the very beginning, programs of work, education and recreation were provided for them. By the summer of 1975 the most innovative of all the programs was underway—*Stretch*. It began with a hearty breakfast that the children themselves learned to prepare in an apartment left vacant for their use. Grits, eggs "any way you want them," sausage, bacon, pancakes—all were on the week's menu. The meal was served in the coffeehouse room where the piano was, so that there could be a time of singing and reflection on the day before the children went to different activities in the basement rooms. Math labs, reading, leatherwork, art, and carpentry workshops were among the activities. On Fridays everyone went on a field trip in the yellow Jubilee bus.

Some of us came to know the children best as we worked in their apartments, and stopped to talk with them. They often made me think of Isaiah's words, "The children born in your bereavement shall yet say in your hearing, 'This place is too narrow; make room for me to live in' " (Isa. 49:20 NEB). They wandered in and out of each other's apartments and seemed to be equally accepted everywhere so that it was hard to know who belonged to which family, and to discover which ones had no beds or food. "Childhood," said Ned Gorman, "is the form that upholds each child's life forever. If a man or a society taints a child's childhood, brutalizes it, strikes it down, and corrupts it with fear and bad dreams, then he maims that child forever, and the judgment on that man and that society will be terrible and eternal."

The people of Jubilee believe this. The truth of it runs through our own troubled feelings and "bad dreams," and in what seems to have gone so grievously wrong in the world. Behind all the programs of Jubilee is an effort to provide such a network of caring and support that families will evoke potentialities and give to children a rootedness that will sustain and nurture the whole of their lives, enabling them to pour forth those lives in love.

Harry Guntrip, a psychoanalyst and writer who has worked all his life with deeply troubled persons, wrote:

If human infants are not surrounded by genuine love from birth, radiating outward into a truly caring family and social environment, then we pay for our failure toward the next generation by having to live in a world torn with fear and hate, full of grossly unhappy people who wreck marriages and friendships and constantly swell the ranks of the deeply disturbed, from unproductive hippies living in a flimsy fantasy world, to criminals, delinquents, and psychopaths. In between are the all too common fanatical adherents of scientific, political, economic, educational, and religious ideologies crying to call or drive us to various types of earthly paradise, and always failing to devote their resources to the one necessary thing, achieving a recognition of the fact that the importance of security for babies and mothers outweighs every other issue. If that is not achieved, everything else we do merely sustains human masses to struggle on from crisis to crisis, from minor to major breakdowns. Today the world may not "keep turning" in spite of our ignorance in these matters much longer. Nor do we want hordes of would-be scientific educators teaching psychology to mothers, for the mother's ability to give her baby a secure start in life "does not depend on knowledge, but on a feeling" that comes naturally if she herself feels secure.[2]

Certainly there is no possibility that mothers will feel secure if they lack the critical minimum of shelter, food, and clothing for their young; but these are not enough, as those of us who have all the essentials will tell you. Each of us needs also to be nurtured in a network of caring, if we ourselves are to be nurturing persons who let our own children go free.

In the weeks that Jenny lay ill, young parents sometimes said in their farewells to each other, "Watch out for your children." Wondering to myself at the time about how one might do this, I thought of some of our children who have marched in the peace demonstrations despite the caution, "They are expecting trouble this time." I remembered, too, the children serving meals to the elderly and visiting among the odd assortment of people who come to the Potter's House for Christmas dinner, and my guess is that these are the children for whom we are caring. They have learned that to the best of one's ability one must hold governments accountable. They have not been given the message that old age is tragic and to be dreaded. They are seeing that one is not an outcast because one is disheveled, or eccentric, or demented. They are learning that every human being is interknitted with every other and is worthy of deep respect. These are the children who are now running through the halls of slum apartments, learning to make friends where ever they find themselves, to feel comfortable in settings not their own. They are the truly privileged children among us, the educated children, the children who will not shrink from feelings, the children who will grow up with arms widespread. We think this is also happening

Stretch began with a hearty breakfast

The program included math labs, reading, leatherwork, art and carpentry

John Williams was a Pied Piper. Would the children follow him across the seas to the land whose music he had taught them?

for the children of the Ritz and the Mozart. Today a teacher who had worked with them three months ago and then had to leave, returned for a visit. She was amazed at the change in the children—how their clamoring and wild demands had subsided and how peaceful they had grown. Hearing her speak had the miraculous effect of taking care of some of our own clamoring and wild demands. The people of the Jubilee mission, along with the children, also grew calmer, less frenzied, more like persons of an inward revolution. Not only have they given a little peace—they have taken a little peace. Each day it seems more possible that those who labor with them will find the One whom we are all seeking.

JUBILEE EXPANDS

In April of 1975 Jubilee acquired for $10,000 another apartment building near the riot corridor of Northwest 14th Street. Tom Nees, the pastor of the First Church of the Nazarene, and a group from his congregation who had worked for fifteen months in the Ritz and the Mozart assumed responsibility for the new building.

"Children are going somewhere and know it, even in the beginning of life" (Robert Coles)

Funds for the ministry were contributed by the Nazarene denomination which in the past had concentrated on more traditional inner-city ministries. Alveda Meneely who, to her own surprise, became the office manager explained that this unlikely development was the result of a conference she had had with her pastor several months before. Having come to the place of feeling that she had to be more seriously on an "outward journey" she had told Tom Nees she would do anything—even scrub floors. "The next day," she said, "he came to me and said, 'I have a job for you.'" Then came her introduction to the Ritz, where she worked for several months scrubbing stoves, refrigerators, and floors. After that she became the office manager of an apartment house that the neighborhood people called the city dump. It got its name from the area behind the building where trash had accumulated over an unknown period. Not only was the exterior of the building knee deep in trash, but the large basement area was full of uncollected garbage. Reflecting on this condition Tom Nees remarked, "If garbage is, as they say, a fair barometer of frustration and anger at management systems that fail to work for the poor, it is evident that this building hasn't worked for a long time."

The roof of Jubilee's new building was so far gone that the owners allowed the top-floor tenants to pay no rent. In exchange for free housing they agreed to put out buckets when it rained and not to call the inspector. The hot water and heating systems were in the same state of disrepair. During the winter months the forty-eight apartments could have hot water only three hours each day, but tenants raised no complaint lest they be pushed into the ranks of the city's 100,000 homeless.

The Cresthill was, however, more than a sprawl of unlighted halls and deteriorating apartments. Many of the residents had lived there for a long time, and shared a lot of life together. The average income of most of the families living in the Cresthill, like that of those living in the Ritz and the Mozart, was below the poverty level. Moreover, 58 percent of the adults were unemployed or on public assistance, and of the 42 percent who were working, many on construction jobs or doing day work did not have secure jobs. Perhaps because of the plight in which the tenants found themselves, they knew a sense of community in the building. The resident managers were Walter and Sheila Royster, two very special people who had worked against overwhelming odds to keep the building livable. They listened to the story of Jubilee and immediately took the risk of believing that the people of Jubilee might be genuinely concerned persons. They called on all the tenants, explained the change in ownership, and shared with them the vision of Jubilee. As a result the tenants turned out to help with the removal of the trash and supported

The "City Dump"

Ribbon cutting ceremony at the Cresthill

Jubilee when it presented a proposal to a local community organization. This kind of participation enabled relationships to be established faster and the work to move ahead more rapidly than would have otherwise been possible. Walter Royster, an excellent construction worker, was employed to supervise various facets of the program.

Additional funds still have to be raised before the roof of the Cresthill is replaced, but the feeling is that one day the building will have its new roof, and that the people will live in apartments that are warm and dry. In the meantime the work and waiting goes on in a wholly different atmosphere. This is surprising in view of the fact that many of the physical conditions have changed very little. The people still have to cope with pipes that burst and plumbing that won't work. Garbage, still put out at the wrong time, is occasionally strewn all over the halls by the children. Rats are still there, although their number is diminishing and they do not seem as confident of their rights. The cockroaches move on from the apartment being cleaned and painted to the next apartment, where matters become worse because that tenant now has, in addition to his own, the roaches that were in his neighbor's place. Despite all this something new has been injected into the picture and there is hope. We have all changed a little so that we do not look at each other in quite the same way. Many of us have a whole new understanding of how great is the struggle of the city's poor. We are no longer taking excursions into the ghetto areas to work with them. The people living there have become "our people." It is a matter of going to be with "our kinsmen," and finding ways to join them in their work of liberation.

More than this, the work in the Cresthill is demonstrating that the mission of Jubilee can be duplicated in other places and that congregations can encourage and support each other. It may even be that some of the transformation that the churches so desperately need will take place. With the support and confirmation of his congregation Tom Nees resigned his position as pastor of the First Church of the Nazarene to begin with some members from that congregation and the tenants of the Cresthill a new inner-city church committed to offering decent housing at submarket rentals to those who otherwise would not have it. The effort has the backing of the entire Nazarene denomination and many of the Cresthill tenants, and one has the distinct feeling that a wind is rushing through it all. In any case, the joy of the new congregation is hard for its members to keep within neat bounds. They are now taking up two collections on Sunday in accordance with an old Wesleyan tradition. The first is channeled through church books and dispensed according to established procedures. The second offering is turned over to a person

Resting from labor

in the congregation who is charged to give it to the poor before the week is over.

One of the programs of the new congregation will be the development of a work/study program whereby students may receive academic credit for time spent with Jubilee, the purpose being to help prepare them for careers in urban ministries. A curriculum has already been approved by Eastern Nazarene College in Boston, Massachusetts, the Nazarene Theological Seminary in Kansas City, Missouri, and the Washington International College. While members of the mission are working through the development of the year-round program, students are coming for shorter periods to work in the renovation of the apartments. In the meantime plans go forward for the acquisition of more apartment buildings and the conversion of the present ones into tenant-owned cooperatives.

"One of the best confirmations of our efforts came this week," said Tom Nees,

Wes Michaelson and Tom Nees share ministry with John Perkins of Voice of Calvary

"when I was stopped on the street in front of the Cresthill by the agent who collects the rent in several deteriorated buildings across the street from us. It seems that the people in the neighborhood have been talking to him about what is happening at the Cresthill. The tenants of his building sent him to us to ask whether we would be interested in buying that building too. We do not know that this will be possible, but at least the changes are noticeable when tenants of other buildings begin to invite us in."

Growing stronger in us is the conviction that it might literally be possible for the people of the city to be engaged in the rebuilding of the city, which is the only way it is ever going to be done. Some of us have radically restructured our own time, and we see this happening for others. Our whole list of priorities is changing. Jim Hall, a young research doctor said,

> With customary Yankee economy I converted my uncle's old medical bag into a first-rate tool bag. I must say that I took a special delight in people's reaction as I rode the bus down to Jubilee with my "tool bag" in one hand and a saw in the other. Almost two years later I find myself considering the possibility of scraping the paint off that old bag, cleaning it out, and putting it back to its original purpose. A number of things have happened to account for this: seeing a woman dizzy and with headaches from high blood pressure because she hadn't gotten back to the doctor for a prescription refill, hearing a challenge from one or two of my mission group members to take responsibility for the medical dimensions of the Jubilee call to the poor and the oppressed, awakening to a new understanding of compassion through sharing in the life of a friend who daily visits sick and broken and forgotten people.
>
> A few months ago I turned down offers to join the faculty of several medical schools and pursue a career in research teaching, and pathology at a university center. Instead I chose to stay for an additional year at my present work with the possibilities of being involved in a medical ministry to the poor.

While some pondered matters of vocation, others of us returned once more to matters of lifestyle—how much money to spend on food, housing, and clothing—in other words, matters of consumption, competition and envy. Only now the conversations were more animated, more filled with adventure and less weighted by guilt. We seemed to talk more about what we would be gaining rather than what we would be giving up.

All the while others are coming to join the Jubilee Mission, and it begins to seem possible that churches from the outer city might join with churches from the inner city, rich churches with poor churches and that after three buildings have been restored, there may be another, and another, and another until the whole city has been reclaimed. "You shall be called Rebuilder of broken walls, Restorer of houses in ruins" (Isa. 58:12 NEB).

RAM'S HORN FEASTS

One of the marks of all community, whether it be a community of two or twenty, is the desire to sit down and eat together. So it is with the community of Jubilee. In its second year it began to gather every other week at the Potter's House for an evening that begins with a common meal followed by prayer and celebration. The meal is usually served by the children of the Ritz and the Mozart who have formed a Ritzart Baking and Catering Service and beg for chances to use their new arts. The occasions have come to be called Ram's Horn Feasts after the ram's horn that was sounded to herald the beginning of the Jubilee Year. It was actually a blast from the ram's horn that caused the walls of Jericho to fall. Always the great trumpet was sounded to proclaim a new and happier era for Israel. The people of Jubilee have this same proclamation in mind for the oppressed of the nation's capital. They are convinced that all the walls that stand in the way of a better life for people housed in tenements, in filthy inhuman jails, overcrowded mental institutions, and dilapidated nursing homes will be brought down, and the people shall walk into a new land where there is color and light, plenty of space, and singing, caring people. A litany of the Ram's Horn Feast reads:

We are a believing people: we believe that God loves all the bound people of this city.

We are a pleading people; we will plead with God to save our city as Abraham pleaded for Sodom.

We are a sharing people:
We will try to be ourselves what we long for our whole city to be—a people sharing our resources so that no one is in need.
Each of us brings our few loaves and fishes.
We are an adventuring, bold people: together we will tackle the worst areas of need in the city, one of which is slum housing.

Together we will discover what it means to be servants of Jesus Christ and servants of the city.

The community that gathers for the Ram's Horn Feast is made up of a great diversity of persons—the old, the maimed, the halt, the educated and not so educated. Some are successful, some are so-called "dropouts." A few like to speak in intellectual terms, and a few like to speak in tongues. We are from churches housed in storefronts and from churches with impressive towers. In all, we make a strange company, but that is the way we want it to be. We meet to celebrate our common humanity and to read and ponder Scripture and to wait for the empowering of the Spirit.

The people of the Ram's Horn Feasts share the common spirit of hope which is at the heart of the liberation movement going on all over the world today. They believe that God acts with men and women whenever they move out in love for the neighbor. Their spirit is quite different from the one of foreboding that grips so many groups today who feel that the world is moving toward disaster—that what we are witnessing is the demise of a civilization, the breakdown of our societies. Is the latter the true assessment of our times, or are we sensing the signs of Pharaoh's household breaking up—small groups of people setting out to build a new society? To be sure, the poor grow poorer, but they no longer accept this fact with resignation. Across the globe one hears new voices raised. Hundreds of newsletters and small publications take up the cries of the oppressed, small numbers of the elite pass over to their side, and here and there a Moses figure stands out.

At the Ram's Horn Feasts we do a lot of talking about houses, and community building, and a world that is divinely marked for salvation. The other night, after the simple meal had been eaten and the tables cleared, we each drew the floor plan of the houses where we had lived as children, so that we might know each other better, and understand better how houses had shaped our own histories for better or for worse. When we had made our rough sketches we took the others at our tables through a tour of the rooms. After that a few volunteered to share their houses with everyone. Hyib's house was a one-room thatched dwelling in a compound in Africa. Close by was another one-room house where his father lived and where he and his brothers went for their meals. Also nearby was another house where his mother, the first wife of his father, lived, and close to that was the house of his "small mother," the second wife of his father. Esther's house was a two-story farmhouse in Virginia where every room was graced with the memory of a gentle and teaching father. Then there was the house of Louise Stewart, which was a one-room log cabin. "My father was shot in that room when I was three," she said. When asked

The people of Jubilee

The Rev. George Davis shares the
Jubilee mission

A partner in the Ritzart Baking and
Catering Service

"Why?" she simply replied, "It was over ten cents. My father was shot for ten cents."

On other nights we discussed the possibility that the people in the Ritz and the Mozart might buy the apartments in which they lived with no down payment, and we considered the gifts that each of us might use to open up the way. A member of Jubilee said, "We are not looking for miracles to come from outside ourselves. We believe that each of us has something to give to the struggle."

Reverend Davis of the King Emanuel's Baptist Church said, "We have to help more people to know that they are children of God, that the world is not acceptable as it is, and that we can change it. There is a promised land, and we can all move into it. We simply have to stay on our knees and keep our arms outstretched. This is the only proper posture for Jubilee. Only if we act, and ask, and listen are we going to find out what He is trying to tell us."

As the weeks go on it is clear that Jubilee—more than a housing project—is a people caught up in a movement with a long history. "Go and tell Pharaoh, King of Egypt, to set the Israelites free." When we stand back and look at them the people of Jubilee seem a bit ragged and sometimes pathetically small in number for so large a task as the restoration of a city. But then they have a ram's horn and, as everyone knows, that is no ordinary trumpet, but one with the power to create supernatural effects. Gordon Cosby keeps telling the people of Jubilee, "We have available to us the insurmountable power of Christ, and we can claim some of that power." At the same time it is abundantly clear that this other realm of power is not power as the world knows it, but a power that comes through the emptying of one's self, from putting aside the usual patterns of leadership, acceptable norms of achievement, divesting one's self of influence and position, and taking up the role of servant.

We sometimes hear these as harsh demands. It is one thing to work for change in the world and another to work for change in one's self. If we each have in us the oppressed—the wretchedly poor that needs something for itself, and takes up the cause of the poor "out there"—we also have in us the oppressor who turns from the role of servant, who trusts in other forms of power, and does not mind holding another down on his own way up. After all, when we are wise, and educated, and healthy, and know who we are, and are in places of influence, we will be so much better able to do good and dispense light and help. We do not want to suspect about ourselves what we would much rather believe to be true about others. It is easier to identify with the helpless victims of society, and to be outraged over their plight, than to find in ourselves the one who keeps in bondage or crushes the spirit of others, or simply withholds the confirmation that another needs.

Unfortunately, we each have both the oppressed and oppressor in us—evil as well as good. This is probably what Nietzsche meant when he said, "Never does man lie more than when he's indignant." This is why the people of Jubilee struggle not with the building of a movement, but the building of a community. We know that we do not fight the evil one alone. The forces of demonic power are too great. We need each other. We have lived too long under Pharaoh's rule. He has fathered us, and if we are to break away from him, and free ourselves of his ways that we have all unconsciously taken as our ways, we will need help each day in surrendering to Jesus Christ. He is the Divine Comrade who, when we ask, will tell us the way to go. He is the gateway to the release of the Holy Spirit. God's revolutionary movement has always had as its basis the small liberating community whose members know enough about themselves to engage in their own struggle for freedom.

4 Education for a New Society

The Lord God has given me
the tongue of a teacher
and skill to console the weary
with a word in the morning;
he sharpened my hearing
that I might listen like one who is taught.

Isa. 50:4 NEB

In his *Asian Journal* Thomas Merton wrote about his meeting with the Dalai Lama, the religious head of the Tibetan Buddhists. Each was eager to learn what the other could teach him about the religious life. The Dalai was particularly interested in Western monasticism and the vows that the monks made. At first Merton did not know what the Eastern man of prayer was asking. Then the Dalai Lama said: "Well, to be precise, what do your vows oblige you to do? Do they simply constitute an agreement to stick around for life in the monastery? Or do they imply a commitment to a life of progress up certain mystical stages?"

Merton reports that he hemmed and hawed a bit, and said, "Well, no, that's not quite what the vows are all about." He was arrested, however, by the fact that this is what the spiritual director of Tibetan Buddhists thought the vows *should* be. Reflecting on the matter later he came to the conclusion that this was exactly the concern of monasticism. He wrote: "When one stops and thinks a little bit about St. Benedict's concept of *Conversio morum,* that most mysterious of our vows, which is actually the most essential, I believe it can be interpreted as a commitment to a total inner transformation of one sort or another—a commitment to become a completely new man. No matter where one attempts to do this, that remains the essential thing."[1]

When I reflect on the Tibetan monk's question as it pertains to the vows that we make as members of the Christian community, I also come to Merton's understanding. The vows that we make when we become members of the Church of

Jesus Christ are more than an oath to stick around with a particular group of people. I believe that they can be interpreted as a commitment to a total inner transformation. "The only thing that counts is new creation!" (Gal. 6:15 NEB).

This transformation which takes place as we try to live out our lives with those who are also called to be on this same inward path, is simply learning to live by love—learning to be persons in community with other persons. This is the most creative and difficult work to which any of us will ever be called. There is no higher achievement in all the world than to be a person in community, and this is the call of every Christian. We are to be builders of liberating communities that free love in us and free love in others.

I have a friend, Wes Michaelson, who has been for a number of years an assistant to a senator and a political writer. Whenever we meet our favorite subject is the church. I think we always talk about the same things because when it comes to a time of reflection, Wes likes to say, and I like to hear him say, "The ultimate political act is the creation of community." I believe this. The building of community is the ultimate revolutionary act. Christ did not simply tell us to love one another. He "acted out" what he was talking about, striving with twelve to create a miniature model of the community he was foretelling. Community energizes, injects spirit, sends out waves of hope, attracts, and finally disturbs ordinary patterns of thinking and responding, which is the reason an authentic expression of community often threatens the established order and in time finds itself in opposition to existing powers.

The vocation of Christians is to be builders of communities that join them with what is highest in themselves, within another and within the whole human race. The most basic thing that Jesus does when he liberates us is to make us caring people who then have the commission to build communities in the places where we live and play and work. No matter how much caring one individual receives from another, it is never enough for healing. Each of us needs a variety of people and diverse experiences over a long period of time if we are to move toward wholeness —the inner transformation that Merton talks about. Communities of caring are necessary not only for adults, but for children. If we can give children the experience of community they will not have our same difficulties in becoming builders of community. In my mail one day came a letter from a young father who is a mental health clinician:

> There are some areas of your community that I would hope to see developed, such as the place of children in your small mission group structure. It is essential that children

experience adult models in all areas of life. With the small group one can touch and observe the pulse of the life process. Children have to experience that at a meaningful level. Children need to have meaningful relationships with many different adults for their own maturation. I think there is much in favor of family cluster-type relationships as a natural extension of the small group life.

No single relationship, no matter how cherished, is adequate for the nurturing of a person. Therefore, communities of caring and thus of hope must be built in our despairing age. For this to happen the churches must consider the matter of their own transformation, so that their structures do not contradict their revolutionary gospel or prevent the "acting out" of that gospel in small faith communities. The help that we need lies in that first model of a liberating, healing community. If we can try to understand its message anew for our own lives and our own age, perhaps we too can make of our churches underground seminaries for the releasing of spirit in persons. Christ was ever teaching the twelve how to live together—how to relate to one another and to God, and pointing them toward that day when they would themselves be the founders of faith communities.

A book that captured the attention of my community this past year was Bruno Bettelheim's, *A Home for the Heart.* We found in its pages a contemporary model of the healing community toward which we were striving. The book is the story of a revolutionary doctor who, with his colleagues, broke with classic and rigid institutional controls in order to lead to freedom "incurable" schizophrenic and autistic children. *A Home for the Heart* is the description of the community that a giant of a man helped to create during twenty-nine years at the Orthogenic School of the University of Chicago. The book is important because, if we can find out what makes the mental institution work, we will know what makes the school, and office, and church work as well as what will make for health in our families.

Page after page unfold a compelling and instructive story of the gradual creation of a healing atmosphere, the building of a "home for the heart." Not only the patients, but the staff, from head therapist to janitor and cook, are persons on a pilgrimage.

Dr. Bettelheim believes passionately in a philosophy of "total milieu therapy." Room furnishings, art, and even tableware are important in the school's total treatment design. Architecture and decor help to create or destroy spirit. Glass and real china are used, because plastic tableware might give the young patients the silent message that they cannot be trusted with breakable dishes.

The most important task of therapy at the Orthogenic School "is not to have the

All of us need a variety of people and diverse experiences if we are to move toward wholeness

Students from many cultures living in the Ritz apartments take time off from renovation work to talk about global community with a member of the National Academy of Science

patient gain insight into his unconscious, but to restore him to a high degree of justified self-esteem."

Every child and worker at the school is a part of the decision-making process that might affect his or her life. No matter how sick a child is, the staff exercises a reverent respect for that child's autonomy and capacity to make life-affecting decisions. How much anger would go out of the world and how much spirit would flow into it, if this same amount of respect were exercised in our dealings with functioning adults. After a number of preadmission visits to the Orthogenic School each child is asked if he wishes to come to the institution. This fateful decision is often given into the hands of children who cannot or will not talk.

> Though he may have declared his wish to come earlier, we ask him again to make sure he has not changed his mind. Even mute patients have their own ways of informing us whether they wish to enter an institution. For example, when asked whether they prefer to stay or to leave, some simply remain sitting—or resist leaving in some other way. On several occasions I have had such experiences with mute patients. When I had asked them this question and given them considerable time to reflect and react, after ten minutes or so of silence, I said that since they didn't respond I could only conclude that they wished to leave. Opening the door of my office, I suggested they do so. One patient got up and carefully closed the door; two others slammed it shut with a big bang—in all three instances the patient then sat down with a satisfied expression. One mute patient had sat rigidly through all the visits, as if "at attention," despite all our efforts to make him relax. When we asked him whether he wanted to live with us or return home, he suddenly relaxed, and stretching out on a couch pretended to fall asleep.[2]

This is a story I want to keep in mind as I walk through the days of my own life, and struggle to create for myself and for others a small liberating community. Part of me does not want to be responsible in the making of decisions and would gladly give them over to someone else. On the other hand, another part of me feels that it knows best what is good not only for myself but for others, especially when those others are sick, or uneducated, or poor, or inexperienced. How do we strengthen and preserve in ourselves the faculty of free consent, and cherish and honor it in others? Praise be to God for all those gentle souls who model for us the new creation.

On every page of Dr. Bettelheim's book one finds help and instruction for the creation of a healing community, for the mental patient is not that different from the so-called normal person. His world is like an enlarged photograph of ours that gives us a better look at our own hopes and needs and fears, at what we do to ourselves, or will not allow ourselves. Of all the wise passages in this great man's book I return most often to the following because it gives me perspective for the times when I am in my own pit, and instruction for the times when I lie down in green pastures but my friend is in her pit:

The mental patient lives as if in a deep, dark hole without exit, imprisoned there both by his anxieties and by the insensitivities of others which he views as inimical designs. We have to invent and construct a way for him—let's say a ladder. We have to build this from our own past; our knowledge; our personality; and our understanding of the patient; but most of all through our empathy that tells us which unique, and uniquely human, ladder will be suitable for this particular patient. Contrary to his old convictions that there is no exit, the patient must first come to believe that on this ladder he can climb out of his prison, and then eventually try to do so. To bring this about, it must be possible for him to watch us work long and hard putting together this ladder, which must be very different from all others that have ever existed before. The patient will try to destroy the ladder, convinced for a long time that we do not fashion it to help him climb to liberty, but only to induce him to move into a worse prison (which we wish him to enter for some unfathomable reason that will benefit us more than him, and which may only project him into more dangers). After all, the patient knows his old prison, as terrible as it is, and somehow has learned to protect himself against its most painful features through his symptoms. Those symptoms—his protective devices—he knows we want him to relinquish. How can he trust us who have such evil designs? He also will try to dismantle the ladder in much the same way as the child destroys the toy whose nature he wishes to understand.

We will have to climb down into the hole where the patient vegetates on this ladder of empathetic understanding, while the patient tries to destroy it if for no other reason than to test our determination.

If the patient decides that he does not wish to use this avenue of escape offered to him, we must accept and respect such a decision—without stopping our efforts to be with the patient in his now no longer inescapable, but self-chosen abode, so that at least he won't dwell alone in his misery.[3]

When I am in the darkness of my own prison, I long most for someone who understands what my world and its walls and shadows are all about. This is not to say that we are to confirm each other in our wrong perceptions of persons and events. Diogenes knew the path of healing when he took his lantern in hand and went in search of an honest man. Only our passionate pursuit of truth can ever set us free. I doubt, however, that anyone ever fastens on the belt of truth and takes up the agonies of freedom except in a climate of empathy.

When I ponder how healing comes, I think of Jesus taking the blind man by the hand, and leading him away from curious eyes—out of the village to a private place.

> Then putting spittle on his eyes, and laying his hands on him, he asked, "Can you see anything?" The man, who was beginning to see, replied, "I can see people; they look like trees to me, but they are walking about " (Mark 8:23–24 JB).

The man's reply, indicating such a distorted view of things, could seem to offer appropriate opportunity for Jesus to lecture. But the Scripture says,

> Then he laid his hands on the man's eyes again and he was cured, and he could see everything plainly and distinctly (Mark 8:25 JB).

Always when a person's feelings are hurt, when he has suffered loss or known rejection, things do not look as they are. At such a time honesty is not sufficient to restore another's sight. When we see men as trees, walking—and this happens to everyone at one time or another—then we need one who takes us by the hand, and one who lays upon us a hand.

Elie Wiesel says that, in Hasidism, "Everything becomes possible by the mere presence of someone who knows how to listen, to love and to give of himself." Therein lies the essence of every genuine community of faith. A person is not left alone in his joy, and certainly never in his sorrow. Wiesel tells the story of a contemporary Hasidic rabbi who decided to question his disciple:

> "How is Moshe Yaakov doing?" The Disciple didn't know. "What!" shouted the Rabbi, "You don't know? You pray under the same roof with him, you study the same texts, you serve the same God, you sing the same songs, and you dare to tell me that you don't know whether Moshe Yaakov is in good health, whether he needs help, advice or comforting?"[4]

None of us today can live on any real level of awareness unless we emotionally get hold of the fact that most of the people who appear so calm and assured have an incredible amount of tumult and pain in their lives. Every human being comes into adulthood wounded. Sometimes our wounds are revealed in lack of trust, sometimes in fear or self-centeredness. Our experiences and prejudices and mixed-up learnings give us a wrong impression of what we hear and what we see. The trees that seem like men walking, are a blown-up picture of how we are all seeing things. The prison of our misery is not seeing things as they really are. Learning to love is an extraordinary work because it means dealing with that which has fouled up our perception of reality, recovering from injured self-esteem, getting in touch with the hidden streams of healing that flow at the center of our own beings, so that we can drink of those secret waters and be whole.

No one wants to give simplistic answers to the complex issue of housing, decaying cities, and hunger. We cannot name the name of Christ and not be somewhere concretely involved working for the solution of those problems. Whatever we do, however, must be done with an ever-deepening consciousness that the people inside the churches and the people outside the churches are asking in epidemic proportions the question, "Am I loved?" The threat to world community, community in the small group, and community between groups, is the pervasive anxiety and hostility that have been created in the lives of so many who have heard no satisfying answer to that most poignant of questions. When almost everyone is asking the same question, there are not enough to make answer. If I am busy wondering whether I am approved and received, I do not see your plight as you wonder about these same things.

The poet and rabbi, Sigmund Freud, was trying to give us some understanding of our situation when he wrote that we are threatened with suffering from three directions: from our bodies which are doomed and whose aches and pains remind us even now that we will die; from the structures of society—the external order which can rage against us; and from our relations with one another. "The suffering," he added, "which comes from this last source is perhaps more painful than any other."[5]

We have already been wounded by our relationships with others when we hear that impossible call to be a builder of community. Jesus was aware of this. In his life with the twelve he gives a healing-teaching model. His understanding of our situation is perhaps best revealed in that extraordinary statement, "It is not the healthy that need a doctor, but the sick; I did not come to invite virtuous people, but sinners" (Mark 2:17 NEB). The first step on the spiritual path is the understanding that all is not well with one's life. The eleventh-century Abbot, Adam of Perseigu, must have thought so because he came to the idea that one went to a monastery primarily to be cured. After a period of healing and convalescence, one was ready to be educated in a new way—to be educated as a New Being. This same observation surely applies to the Church. We go there first to be cured and then to be educated in a new way. If our churches are to be liberating communities, and we are to be members and founders of liberating communities, then each of us must do an extraordinary inward work.

An important dimension of this inward work—the education of the new person

—is that we learn to give attention to our feelings, learn to educate them and to care for them. We know a lot about educating the mind, but very little about educating feelings. In fact, very few people know that feelings can be educated, or that the state of our feelings determine the state of our relationships. Our schools treat students as though they had only minds—no feelings. We help young people to develop the capacity to think for themselves, but not the capacity to feel for themselves. We do not recognize, or we ignore the fact that the human mind is powerfully influenced by the emotional life. Our actions and our decisions are being determined by feelings that are still in a primitive stage. The result is that humankind has accomplished towering intellectual feats in every area of life, but we do not have the comparable emotional development needed for the enormous responsibility of handling ourselves or the machinery we have created. Our whole civilization is threatened by the division that exists between mind and heart. If we do not bridge the gulf between our feelings and our intellect we will fall into the yawning chasm between them. Dr. Bettelheim, reflecting on the concentration camps of Nazi Germany, wrote, "The heart can no longer afford to have reasons the mind knows not of." Not only are our feelings wounded, but whole emotional areas of our lives are waiting to be formed. The only time we receive any real help with feelings is when the pain of them is so acute that we are compelled to seek help in understanding what they are trying to tell us.

In America we speak about the terrible pressures of public office. If we lived in an age of enlightenment we would encourage our public officials to be in some kind of therapeutic relationship with another human being who would give them a sheltered place in which to reflect aloud on their feelings and thoughts. But that is an unknown idea. As it is, we have so little understanding of emotional needs and the evolutionary journey that we look askance at any public person who admits his need for help in exploring his inner life. We do not allow our public servants to be pilgrims. We almost make certain that the affairs of our land will be conducted out of the unconscious.

If the churches could recover their own roots, become Christian again, we could begin the struggle to provide for ourselves and for others an atmosphere in which our feelings would be released from their terrible bondage. We could give our energies to the creation of soul and spirit in persons. We could recover the fire and passion and motivation for good that can come only through the emotions. This is neither to put aside the intellectual nor to detract in any way from its significance. The heart must be informed by the mind, and the mind by the heart. I wonder whether there can be any correspondence between the two—any healing of the division between mind and heart—unless we treat them as equals, giving as much attention to the release of our feelings as we give to the release of our minds. Love is after all an emotion, and religion has to do with a revolution of love in the world. That revolution cannot take place until our churches take seriously the matter of their own transformation and begin to educate for a new community.

The proper studies of any church are the New Testament, the Old Testament, the child, the man, the woman. Very little is known about the whole developmental process. If Christianity is about freeing people, making choices, being liberators, then it is not appropriate to entrust the area of growth and change to a few experts outside the church whose services will be available to only the few. We need to change our church schools into underground seminaries having as their revolutionary task the creation of studying-healing-research programs that will educate us for freedom.

This past year my own small group worked with the designing and structuring of new classes for the Church of the Saviour's School of Christian Living. We had observed that most of the people in our school, though they were middle class, young, rich in gifts and personality, were suffering people. They were also for the most part people who had taken the first step in spirituality. They knew that all was not well with their lives. In preparation for our work we studied *Home For The Heart*. We wanted to use as many of Dr. Bettelheim's concepts as possible in our own school so that it could be a temple of healing from which people might go forth to be healers in their own small communities of family, office, and church.

A CLASS IN CHRISTIAN COMMUNITY

For a class in Christian Community we designed exercises that would help us to experience some of the things that we were setting forth as the marks of the new community. For each class we structured times of silence so that the students could be in touch with their feelings about, and responses to what was happening in the class. We followed each group experience with a time for centering and reflection, being thoroughly convinced that one of the important ways to learn emotionally is through reflection. We tried to help one another to be aware that we were teachers as well as learners. Whenever we saw a person in a pit we gave our hearts and minds to the construction of a ladder.

We tried to live out among ourselves and in the midst of the class the kind of community we were describing. Using the model of the Orthogenic School we put our relationships with each other and with the students under scrutiny. After each

"Childhood is the form that upholds each child's life forever" (Ned O'Gorman)

class, members of our group met for our own time of reflection, to listen to what our feelings were saying to us. We did the painful work of trying to be open with each other—saying when we felt angry, jealous, or competitive in our team teaching. We struggled to learn what our failures and our successes could teach us. All of this was harder work than we had anticipated when we were merely reading about "self-questioning" in Dr. Bettelheim's book. Some sessions increased our feelings of anxiety to such a degree that, when we left each other we wondered why we had decided on so unrewarding a path. We better understood the reasons why the whole area of feelings had been neglected. Yet we did not give up our work—the work of reconciliation. In our larger community we are forever talking about the taking of risk and being willing to fail, but usually we are referring to some program of action. We decided that we wanted to take our risks in the whole area of feelings in order to learn something about transformation and transforming structures. We did not try to hide our struggles from the class members. We let them watch us agonizing, making mistakes, changing our minds, solving differences, practicing what we believed. We tried to be with them persons in community, and now and then the gift of community was given. Always it happened when we made ourselves most vulnerable.

On one class night, in our time of centering, a member of the class slipped to Joan a poem she had written about Jenny. Joan read the poem in the silence and was swamped by waves of grief. She was to lead the study that night, but decided that she would not ignore her feelings and go on as if they did not exist, all "for the sake of the class." Her life was not a show with a scheduled "walk on" time. For her own sake, she said, "I do not feel that I can do what I had planned. Susie gave me a poem she wrote and I am into my sad feelings." We sat for a few moments in the quiet while Joan wept for the child that was no more. Then someone asked if she would like to have the poem read aloud. She said she would, and we listened to the reading of a new "Poem for Jenny," while Joan continued to weep. When the reading was finished a young woman in the class said, "I lost my three-year-old five years ago. In the loss of your child I have lived over again that experience." And then she said to Joan ever so tenderly, "The pain changes, but it does not go away." Joan answered, "I am beginning to know that. I used to think that in two years I would be my old self again. Now I know that time will never be." And then she added, "But that does not keep me from affirming my life and saying that it is good."

The exchange of the two mothers brought to mind words that Freud had written to a friend who had lost a son:

We know that the acute grief we feel after such a loss will come to an end, but we shall remain inconsolable, and never find a substitute. Everything that comes to take its place, even if it were to fill it completely, nevertheless remains something different. And this is really as it should be. It is the only way of perpetuating the love which we do not wish to renounce.[6]

Again we hear that voice in Ramah, Rachel weeping for her children, refusing to be consoled "because they were no more" (Matt. 2:18 NEB).

Half an hour went by before Joan returned to the material that had been scheduled for the session, and then she was talking to a different class than the one which had assembled. We had trusted each other with our feelings, and this is always much more difficult than telling a class that when we join the Christian church we become members of a community that covenants to bear one another's burdens.

While it is true that we have a responsibility for being open to what is happening in the hearts of our brothers and sisters, it is also true that we have some responsibility to let others know how things are with us, if we want their companionship in our joy and in our sorrow. When a person says, "I didn't know that you were in trouble," we cannot reply, "I did not want to bother you. I know how busy you are," or, "If you cared, you would have come without my asking." If we walk through the Christian community hugging our needs to ourselves, it may mean that we do not trust our fellow pilgrims to keep the covenant they have made with us. This is where many of us are, and it is all right to be at that place. If we demand that people share their feelings, our last state will be worse than our first. Trust is built ever so slowly. What so often happens, however, is that we keep not only our feelings to ourselves, but our expectations of one another. When this happens we end up accusers of the community. "I needed you, and you were not there. You did not come." These words so often lie beneath the wounds that fester and corrupt the heart, and over which no healing waters flow. Our secret griefs can become a consuming sickness resulting in demands that no community can meet. Then we begin to ask of others that they be to us what they cannot possibly be, that they do for us what only we can do for ourselves.

The psalmist in his cries of petition is in touch with his real pain. He knows why he suffers, and that is not as easy as most of us have been led to think. He begins, as all true petitioners must begin, "Out of the depths I cry to thee" (Ps. 131:1 RSV). This kind of petitioner does not go away empty-handed. He feels listened to, cared for, and unburdened. His cries become praise of the listening God, whose listening and caring are his healing. The experience of the psalmist was Joan's experience. She declared how it was with her. She spoke out of her depths and the tears were once again wiped away. Everything was "made all right." More than that Joan had not robbed us of our time or our energy. She had helped to restore the years that the locusts had eaten. In that class we were educating hearts and minds about the nature of God and the nature of the community He calls into being. We were learning that we do not ruin everything with our tears. Indeed, our tears can make right all the things that are so terribly wrong.

CLASS ON ANGER

When that class was over, Joan and I designed a seminar course that would help us to look at anger in ourselves—our creative and destructive ways of handling it. We felt that an understanding of anger and its mysterious workings was essential to the building of community, whether it was the community of marriage, the community of our small group life, or community in the city and the world. The increase of violence and apathy in our society seemed ample evidence of our failure to work with this important emotion in our lives. But Joan and I had more than intellectual reasons for taking up so large a subject. We were both dealing with our own feelings of abandonment, helplessness, hurt, and rage. We were more than eager scholars. We each had a work of reconciliation to do in our hearts.

Our reading list for the seminar included works by Freud, Jung, Horney, Lorenz, Rochlin, Grier, Fanon, and others. We had the feeling that we were beginning a lifelong inquiry and that an informed mind was the proper foundation for that search. While the seminar was a discussion/reading program, we wanted our companions also to be researchers. A desire to explore in one's self and to share findings, as well as to engage in a serious study of literature on the subject were set as prerequisites for attendance. Enrollment was limited to twelve.

Behind our offering of the course was another strong motivation. We felt that not very much was known about the whole subject of anger or, for that matter, about any other important emotion. While it was fairly well known that anger lay behind anxiety, apathy, withdrawal, indifference, and depression and all kinds of common diseases, the average person had been given little encouragement to uncover this emotion and to work creatively with it. We were convinced that humankind as a whole was on the frontier of understanding the emotional life, and that the lack of significant progress was due to our failure to engage ordinary persons from all walks of life in an exploration of their own feelings. Though we did not assume that any of us had Freud's or Jung's genius for discovery or capacity for making penetrating observations, we nonetheless felt that these faculties could be developed. Moreover, the fact that we had available to us the whole body of literature left by these two giants as well as all the writings that came after them would more than make up for our clinical inadequacies. We also took heart for our adventure from the knowledge that so many of the trained explorers of depth psychology quoted not their own colleagues, but writers, philosophers, and theologians such as Dostoevski, Nietzsche, and Kierkegaard.

The more we considered anger, the more appropriate the subject seemed. We were, after all, possessors of the biblical injunction, "Be angry, but do not sin; do not let the sun go down on your anger" (Eph. 4:26 RSV). We did our study against the backdrop of that Scripture. Most of us, knowing what was in us, realized that we were far from living up to its command. Within the class we seemed to fall into two distinct groups. Those who felt that they were not enough in touch with their anger, or were too afraid of it to "be angry," and at the other end of the spectrum those who felt the sun was setting every day on their anger. For them anger was an explosive emotion whose reins they were not holding. They wanted to be able to exercise choice over its expression.

We made our way through the books on anger, though a few us found ourselves reluctant scholars. With each reading assignment we had the instruction to observe anger in ourselves. We tested all readings against our own history, keeping before us the question, "Does the writer's observation ring true in my own experience?" Each week in the class we accepted the intellectual discipline of coming to grips as a group with the main points of an author, and then we shared our personal findings. Many of the writers conceived of anger as a form of energy that will not just go away. If we do not use the energy of anger in constructive activities, or for our growth, or to redress wrongs, it will build up in us until one day it erupts in violent and sometimes dangerous ways, or turns inward to destroy us. Anger held too far back in our unconscious finds its expression in illness and disease. In subtle ways it will destroy the relationships that we so desperately need for any enduring conviction of our own worth. As the psalmist discovered, we do not always have the power to choose not to express our anger:

> I said: I will keep close watch over myself
> that all I say may be free from sin.
> I will keep a muzzle on my mouth,
> so long as wicked men confront me.

In dumb silence I held my peace,
    so my agony was quickened,
    and my heart burned within me.
My mind wandered as the fever grew,
    and I began to speak (Ps. 39: 1–3 NEB).

Our chances of controlling anger and thus using it in constructive, creative ways for the building of community are greatly increased if we discern its clamoring voice and do not wait until a fever has grown in us to give it expression.

Almost every week we worked with a Scripture that expressed strong emotion. We pondered psalms and the incident of Jesus and the moneychangers. We roleplayed the story of the prodigal son, and the conflict between Mary and Martha. For one assignment we did an analytical study of the angry young man called Moses of whom it was written, "He looked this way and that, and seeing no one he killed the Egyptian and hid him in the sand" (Exod. 2:12 RSV). What were the events of his childhood that had given him such a strong identification with the oppressed and so hurt him that all his life he struggled with his own anger? "I took the two tablets and flung them down and shattered them in the sight of you all" (Deut. 9:17 NEB).

It was an angry Moses that Michelangelo freed from marble. Sigmund Freud, the contemplative, wrote a long composition on the Moses of Michelangelo:

For no piece of statuary has ever made a stronger impression on me than this. How often have I mounted the steep steps of the unlovely Corso Cavour to the lonely place where the deserted church stands, and have essayed to support the angry scorn of the hero's glance! Sometimes I have crept cautiously out of the half-gloom of the interior as though I myself belonged to the mob upon whom his eye is turned—the mob which can hold fast no conviction, which has neither faith nor patience and which rejoices when it has regained its illusory idols."[7]

Later in his piece on the statue Freud concludes that the sculptor has added

something new and more than human to the figure of Moses; so that the giant frame with its tremendous physical power becomes only a concrete expression of the highest mental achievement that is possible in a man, that of struggling successfully against an inward passion for the sake of a cause.[8]

In his book, *Man's Aggression,* Dr. Gregory Rochlin stated over and over the theme that whatever lowers self-esteem increases hostility. Anger is an energy that comes to our assistance to help us implement change, to restore ourselves. One of the ways our class worked with this concept was to break down into groups of four and to make a list of experiences in life that might injure self-esteem. The list in my small group read:

Any physical illness or handicap
Physical appearance
Feeling of helplessness
An unacceptable family member
Unacceptable friends
Failures
Disappointments
Unreal expectations
Loss through death
Rejection
Demands
Disapproval
Lack of recognition
Physical deprivation—food, housing, clothes

We then listed the events for each seven-year developmental period of our lives that might have injured our self-esteem and contributed to that private storehouse of our own anger, and events for the same period that had made us feel good about ourselves. We shared these historical experiences with each other.

We learned that our self-esteem has not only been damaged by large events, but is hurt each day in small encounters. Dr. Rochlin helped us to see that we are hardly aware of the effects of humiliation on the course of our personal lives, let alone of its influence on the fate of the whole human society. One of his major themes is that injured self-esteem can be restored only through our work and through our relationships. Both are important.

The intelligent work, the creative act, the kind overture, in and of themselves, do not accomplish the endless task of self-confirmation. We require social approval and support for our very being.[9]

If I have work of great meaning and scope to do, but my relationships are not satisfactory, I am a person in trouble. Conversely, if my relationships are warm and satisfactory, but I have no meaningful work to do, I am a person in trouble. Until I find my vocation I have energy that has not found its flow. Love and work are essential to any feeling of well-being. When we have both, Spirit courses through us. The church is engaged in the education of the New People when it is helping us to form satisfying relationships and helping us to identify gifts, to hear call, to discover vocation. As for a child, we must remember that his play is his work—the way that he explores his inner conflicts, handles his fears, and molds his world a little closer to his own wishes.

The great difficulty encountered in our endeavor to restore self-esteem—both our own and others—is that it can be damaged by our own self-hate and the burdens we place upon ourselves, as well as by the fact that others do not seem to value and enjoy us or need what we have to give. Another large dilemma underscored by Dr. Rochlin is that "when our self-esteem is felt to be jeopardized, it may bring out a tenacious clinging to infantile wishes which may have been long since repressed and even abandoned."[10]

Robert Coles states a similar observation in this way:

> When we are tired, scared or ill, old troubles come back, not to haunt us, or cause us to be called "neurotic," but because we have within us what we *were* as well as what we *are,* and what we hope to be or fear becoming.[11]

Some serious study of these thoughts might help us to extend to ourselves not only some divine mercy, but also caring, in periods of our own regression. If we can grow in understanding of our pain, there may be formed in us the compassion that we need to be builders of caring communities.

Anger has the same root as anguish, and grievance the same root as grief. But how often do we treat an angry person as a person in anguish? How often do we respond to someone with a grievance as a person grieving? Some in our class knew well that anger fully experienced is a very painful emotion. The sage of the Wisdom Book tells us it is alarming "not to know the cause of your suffering" (Wisdom 17:12 JB).

When the eleven-week seminar was completed, many of us wanted to go on and explore more deeply our own anger. Joan and I invited this class on the bold adventure of trying to be healers to each other. The question was sharply asked, "Are we opening Pandora's box?" When we considered that familiar question, usually intended as a warning, we decided that, if this should prove the case for some, we would still much rather let the evil spirits out and have the opportunity of confronting them. When we reflected further, it seemed extraordinary that anyone would choose to keep them boxed up inside herself. Someone also reminded us that we were not living in some rural area without access to professional help, if we found ourselves in trouble.

One who knew the legend of Pandora's box said that when the lid was raised all the spirits escaped except for Hope, which lay at the bottom. We wondered whether there might be so little hope in the world today because most of us had failed to cast out the evil spirits that afflicted us. A second person said that according to another version of the myth the divinities had heaped their special gifts on Pandora, whose name means all gifts. Hermes, however, had put perfidy into her heart and lies into her mouth.

We were persuaded that we must put lying behind us, and acknowledge emotions of anger and hate. If we could not feel our anger, we knew we could not feel our love. Deep in us we knew that one cannot be selective in blocking off emotions. If the church's liberation movement was about freeing love in persons and a revolution of love in the world, we would have to own our feelings of grief, anger, jealousy, and greed, so that joy, love, caring and generosity might flow. When hate and tears were spent perhaps we would find at the bottom of ourselves love and caring. Perhaps when we lost our fear of our anger, we would lose the fear of our love, and begin to practice that gift about which so little is known. In that class we began timidly to explore our responses to anger, and to face the fact of unreasonable anger. Even though one of the ground rules was the honest expression of our feelings, we found it hard and risky work. Our tradition and education had trained us to keep conflict hidden and our real feelings masked. "If you cannot say something nice, don't say it," and "You are just like your father," are familiar and hostile ways of teaching children not to express anger. We wondered how our households and our society which hold honesty as an important value had managed so effectively to teach us to lie about our feelings. Though none of us had ever lost a friend because we had been angry, most of us clung to the feeling that, if we expressed anger toward anyone, we would be deserted. Rather than have that happen we repressed our grievances and, in one way or another, we walked out on our friends. In the beginning most of us felt anxious and uncomfortable when anger was expressed by any member of the group. We also felt anxiety and guilt if we let a class member know that we ourselves were angry. We often discussed the wisdom of always being honest about our feelings.

Once again we made the discovery that we all do not have the same needs. Some needed to be more open in the expression of their feelings, while others needed to learn that they do not have to tell all—that we share with each other because we want to, not because we *ought* to. A few had had the experience of being in groups where pressure was put on people to share and where people were manipulated into sharing, or where members kept inner tallies on how much or how little sharing others did. We discouraged that kind of comparison. We all have secret places. Being in community does not mean that one's life becomes a public sphere. If a person has a "keep out" sign up, it may mean that he is fearful that there is not enough sensitivity in the group, and that there are people who will trespass where they have not been invited. While we struggle to create a climate in which persons are free to share their feelings, we must never insist on that sharing or make it uncomfortable for a person not to share. Each person has an area which should not be violated. If another grows in trust of me, it is not only because of who he is, but because of who I am. While self-disclosure and honesty can be important to one person they can be destructive to another. Recognition of the reality of this is probably what made the greatest contribution to our putting the lid on all negative feelings. Without care and sensitivity no one can be a responsible member of a group. These are the essential qualities needed in any effective communication. For all of us there will be times when we will choose to sacrifice the expression of our feelings for the sake of another. At those times it is important that we be honest with ourselves about what we are feeling and thinking. Then it will not matter so much if we cannot be open with others. Our difficulty comes when we are in touch with too many people who do not allow the grieving or negative part of ourselves to be expressed. Then the sacrifice becomes too great.

In the group as we grew in self-confidence and in trust, we grew bolder in the exploration of our own feelings and less defensive in our responses. It became easier for us to share our frustrations, discouragements, rejections, and fears. Members of the group often helped us to recognize that injured feelings were behind the anger, or that our anger came from our wrong perception of events. Sometimes we were in search of the lost pain that lay beneath our present anguish.

We began to believe more and more in the priesthood of all believers. We began to ask each other not only, "What did you do with your anger today?" but "What did you do with your love today?" In that class we became prophets and priests to each other. We stopped asking for advice and giving advice and became fellow pilgrims.

Our problem is not that we have been hurt and known suffering, but that we have not known how to use suffering and hurt as means of transformation. In a recent New York *Times* article entitled, "Father and Son," Julius Lester describes his relationship with his son. He does not try to protect his son from the racism of his white schoolmates, but helps him to understand what his friends mean when they nickname him, "Milk Chocolate":

"Your friends are trying to tell you that they know you are not like them."
He denied this angrily and I did not argue, admitting to him that I could be wrong.

He continued to protest, however, long after I thought our conversation was over, and I knew that he was confused and hurt. I said nothing more, for they are his friends and how he reconciles his love for them and their racism is a problem I cannot solve for him. I hurt for him, yet I was pleased. I should've known that white America could be depended on to give my son a feeling of racial identity where I couldn't.

More important, however, was the fact that for the first time I felt his life touch mine, for the lives of blacks are like beads strung on a necklace of pain, and we are linked to each other by that pain, regardless of whatever other differences may exist between us.

If he is to be my son truly, he must know that pain, for it was the pain that shaped the man who became his father. It is the means by which to grow, if one learns how, and I will teach my son to know this pain, not as an experience by which to dehumanize and hate whites, or as a wound by which to pity himself. No, the pain can educate his soul, and oddly, if he explores that black pain deeply enough, he will touch the pain that everyone carries.

Then he will be threaded into another necklace, one that will unite him with everyone, even the racist.[12]

The pain that we do not use to create soul in us will often express itself in unexplainable anger, out of proportion to the events that evoke it. Anger is a stage in suffering, but we can lock ourselves into that stage. If we deny to anger some kind of genuine expression, it seeps into a reservoir of anger which may overflow its banks in destructive ways. The most real expression of anger may be our tears. If we can be fully in touch with the pain in our anger, we may be healed and become healers.

The education of the new man and the new woman cannot be confined to a few hours of a formal program each week. The teaching/healing ministry of the church belongs to its whole life. I have been most instructed by my own community on the occasions of its infant dedications, baptisms, weddings, departure services, and deaths.

At the Potter's House we had an interracial, intercultural wedding which was one of the loveliest marriages I have helped to celebrate. No one tried to deny the reality of the circumstances under which it was taking place. Some of our dominant feelings were acknowledged, hallowed, introduced into the sacrament of the marriage ceremony.

After saying a few words about the cost/tension promise that is inherent in all that we set out to do, Gordon Cosby applied the concept to the marriage that was taking place:

Wendy and Nick are aware of the cost in what they are doing. One of the painful dimensions of that cost is that Wendy's church community and her family cannot join with us. While we are rejoicing and grateful, there are others who, because of their love for Wendy, are knowing grief and pain. They want to be with her and yet they are not here because they do not feel that they can affirm the marriage. We have to look at this today, recognize it and be aware of their pain, Wendy's pain, and Nick's pain.

And then, there is, it seems to me, another dimension to the cost of what is taking place. We have to acknowledge the kind of society in which we live, and that through it runs a deep sort of racism. Everywhere they go this couple will be up against that which is cost. The cost will go on and on, and we need to be able to spell it out, and to recognize that this will be a dimension of their lives. This is part of the cost.

My own dominant feelings, however, and the dominant feelings of this community as I know those feelings, are of happiness and joy. In light of where we are in world history with the global needs and problems we are up against, and with the need we have to live in the new order that is coming into being, I cannot think of anything more exciting than to have two people who love one another and can be a symbol of hope in the world that is struggling to be born. In light of the potential, the cost is not out of proportion. We have talked to them about that cost. In one way or another, we have asked, "Have you thought about this? Have you really worked this through?" They will have to struggle with the cost again and again in the days to come, but now let us rejoice because of the potential and because of the promise, for this is a wondrous thing which is occurring. Here in miniature and in microcosm is that toward which our society needs to move in one form or another.

The church that educates for a new society will live out in its structures what it proclaims. The very structures themselves educate. When our acts mirror our words, they give to our words a transforming power. I remember being invited to talk to a class of children about the nature of the Church and its missionary structures. I decided that the best way to talk about the Church's servant role in society was to tell them something about our own small mission groups. As it turned out, that group of a dozen youngsters among themselves was able to name sixteen of the twenty mission groups. Because their parents were all deeply involved in the programs and activities of the groups, the children also knew intimately the life of many of them. I left that classroom a better informed teacher.

One of our mothers said that at her son's birthday party, he asked that she delay the serving of the refreshments. "We had a disagreement," he explained, "and we haven't settled it yet." A few minutes later she looked in on an earnest group of children who had stopped in the midst of a party to take care of some of their injured feelings. I doubt that my generation will be able as easily to make the incredible journey into the New Land where feelings are readily acknowledged, explored, expressed, and accepted.

Ours may be the assignment to wander in the wilderness where there are no sure landmarks and not enough experienced guides, and to put up a few signs that will enable those who follow to walk into the land that the Lord has shown to us. Some may simply have the task of witnessing to their children that the men in that land are not as giants, but that it is indeed a land flowing with milk and honey.

While anger was the subject of our class, jealousy, envy, and every other emotion need the same hospitality. As our fathers knew, the seven sins will deal us death, if we cannot create in our lives a friendly space where they can be received and understood. Our emotions cannot be repressed, but they can be transformed. We do not have to be afraid. We have been assured that in the Kingdom the lamb and the lion lie down together. It is our evolutionary task to usher in the new earth and the new heaven. What does this mean but that we are to be a people doing the work of trying to relate to one another. Very few are engaged in that work.

STAGES OF LIFE

If the church is to educate for the New Community, and shepherd us on the path toward deep and intimate relationships, we must give equal attention to every stage of life. "Growth is painful," we keep repeating but we never fully believe it. Each stage of life, without asking permission, gives to us larger spiritual and psychological tasks. We used to think that adolescence was the great time of upheaval when an enormous inward work had to be accomplished. Then we became young adults and wondered whether we were strange to want to wander over the whole earth while we wrestled with decision, choice, responsibility, claims, commitment. Later we began to look back and to understand that each period has its work and that the new assignment is always larger than the previous one. Now, those who are in middle age weigh carefully what has gone before and know that youth despairs too quickly for so critical an examination of one's past.

I find that I am awed to be in late adulthood—that next to the last stage of what Eric Erickson calls the "life cycle." Unlike the time of youth it has little feeling of permanency. I reflect more often on old age, trying to interpret its mystery, make some sense of it, so that I will be prepared for its enormous hazards and accomplish its great work.

I do not like the concept of aging that my culture has passed on to me. Even though old age, like middle age, is beginning to receive more attention, only a very few enlightened ones view it as a time of growth and development, and yet any careful observer of the life process, who is also a believer, would know that God did not err in his plan when he created so incredible a stage in life. What seems obvious is that he gives to the old those spiritual tasks that can be accomplished only by those with a lifetime of growing, experiencing, and learning, and a storehouse of inner resources to draw upon. I ask the old about this work of theirs, but they do not answer me. In a class in Keeping a Journal, an old woman reads from her journal: "I do not know why, but my friends and I do not talk of aging or of death. I do not think it is because we are afraid, but because we are ashamed, as though it were something that should not have happened to us."

Eric Erickson says that the generations need each other, but the old in our society are among the most oppressed. Until their place in the scheme of things is fully sensed and acknowledged, we are all lost to each other, which may be the reason I must fight dread and the denial of my own aging.

Robert Coles confirms what my experience tells me—"I see the mind as never really developed, but always developing, in its *essence* developing . . . only when a person's last breath has been taken can his biographer draw psychological conclusions."[13] In the last moment the thief on the cross enters into the Kingdom. In the last moment Judas steps out. Robert Coles asks the basic question: "But will revolution against exploiters settle the issue of exploitation, or must man also learn to raise truly less exploitable men—men who are first of all masters of the human life cycle and of the cycle of generations in man's own lifespace?"[14]

Some clinicians are now saying that each seven years mark a new developmental stage. I believe this. Every seven years I seem to find my own soul in turmoil. I do not find the new without facing myself as I am, and who ever really wants to do this unless it is required? Seven is the sacred number. Through all of Scripture it plays a basic role in the reckoning of the years. Jacob labors seven years to win Rachel, and then must labor another seven. Originally the seventh year was the year of remission when debts were to be canceled. The Jubilee Year is made up of seven sabbatical year periods, plus the fiftieth year. The "seventy" are sent out—seven last words from the cross—seven churches. Seven has come to symbolize wholeness, completeness, the end of a period.

The whole history of the world is divided into "jubilee" periods, cycles of seven. The Passover and the pilgrim Feast of Tabernacles are celebrated for seven days.

Each stage of life holds us on its knees
and gives new instructions in "letting go"

On the seventh day God rests. Perhaps we will not be masters of the human life cycle—fulfill that commitment to a life of progress up certain mystical stages— unless we learn that the seventh day is the Sabbath of the Lord our God. Again the first revolutionary is our model. In his own exile he learned the importance of reflection, learned that in the solitude direction is given, learned transcendence of self, learned that who one is is more important than what one does. Moses was more than the leader of a nomadic people, wresting an existence from land and sea and sky, forging toward new territory. Moses was the founder of a faith community, helping a people to understand that there was something more important than the work of their hands, instructing them on how to reflect on their lives before God, building with them a society marked by a noticeably different quality of caring. When the reports came back that the New Land was flowing with honey Moses heard only what he had known all along—that this was the land of which the Lord had spoken, yet he sat down to wait with a reluctant people, and to teach them while he waited. Some activists say that, in the decision not to take his community into the promised country, Moses gave up his leadership. Others believe that he was unwilling to force obedience and was modeling for us the caring qualities of the New Creation.

If we are to be masters of the human life cycle, perhaps we need more than to keep the Sabbath. Perhaps we need every seven years a seven-day pilgrim feast in which we work with the perils of each new stage, acknowledge its challenge, overcome our fears, and celebrate achievements.

Daniel Williams wrote that all human loves bear the possibility of learning to let go. He says "we must speak of *possibility,* for of all the lessons of love, this is the most difficult."[15] Many never learn it. And yet, when we look back, we discover that the lesson was there to be mastered in every stage of life. No matter how much the odds are against it, we first have to learn to "let go" of parents so that we can become a fully differentiated human being, speaking our own thoughts, feeling our own feelings, offering our own praise. This work begins in childhood and we chip away at it all the years of our lives, for the sins of our parents, our grandparents, and great grandparents have been visited upon us. Then comes the day when we have to learn to relinquish the beloved so that she or he is not manipulated by our desires or needs, but can be free to relate to an inner Voice. After that we have to let go of our children so that they can be on that journey of becoming themselves. All of our lives we are given fresh opportunities to practice "letting go." In every relationship we have to learn to let the other go in order to be ourselves the solitary one, the one alone before God. Each stage of life is preparation for the next. Each stage holds us upon its knees and gives new instructions in "letting go."

The dominant theme of Exodus is "Let my people go so that they may keep my pilgrim-feast in the wilderness" (Exodus 5:1 NEB). God is ever seeking to free us from bondage. He will not bind us even to the good—Himself. He has chosen us, but we are not bound to choose Him. He gives us the inheritance we ask so that we will feel blessed and thus free to discover the way for ourselves. However hard it is, we must do the same for others. We must leave them free not to choose us even when we have chosen them.

The way to fight oppression in the world is to begin leaving the Egypt of our own slavery. Who is the Pharoah in our inner household that will not listen to us when we cry out for life? And who are the people that we in turn seek to bind? What is required of us in order that we may free others to follow their own paths and to be on their own search? How do we avoid keeping those inner ledgers that say "you owe me this . . . and you owe me that . . . all this I have done for you . . .?" Sometimes we discover that we labored for another expecting something in return—

love, a relationship. A frequent means of enslaving another is in keeping her dependent. When we do this we keep ourselves dependent, failing to use the resources of our own lives. In freeing the other, we also free ourselves to keep a pilgrim feast in the wilderness, where, though the land be desert, God comes.

A pilgrim has the double task of being utterly committed to the other, and of utterly freeing the other. Life is relationship, learning to relate to the whole earth and all that is therein. But in the end every cherished person must be surrendered, every familiar place given up, every precious object handed over. All of our dyings are preparation for a final dying; all of our births, preparation for the resurrection. God, who makes our very life dependent upon relationship, wants for himself an ever deepening relationship with us, and that is possible only as we become like him. Our final liberating action is to say, "I lay down my life, that I may take it again. No one takes it from me, but I lay it down of my own accord" (John 10:17–18 RSV).

And what are the marks of the transformed person—the person who feels the unity within himself and feels the unity within the world. I used to think that one would know that person by his peace. He would walk with more assurance than the rest of us, speak prophetic and stirring words, radiate a quiet confidence in the future. Now I wonder if the transformed person might not look a little battered.

> He had no beauty, no majesty to draw our eyes,
> no grace to make us delight in him;
> his form, disfigured, lost all the likeness of a man,
> his beauty changed beyond human semblance.
> He was despised, he shrank from the sight of men,
> tormented and humbled by suffering;
> we despised him, we held him of no account,
> a thing from which men turn away their eyes.
> Yet in himself he bore our sufferings (Isa. 53:2–4 NEB).

Perhaps a mark of change in us will be that, while we strive toward wholeness, we no longer ask what is the look of the transformed person, nor do we cast stones at ourselves or at any of God's pilgrim people.

> Shall the thing made say of its maker, "He did not make me"?
> Shall the pot say of the potter, "He has no skill"? (Isa. 29:15 NEB).

Sometimes during the communion supper when the bread is passed to me, I eat of it, and remembering the words of Christ, "Do this in remembrance of me," I pass the bread on to my neighbor and instead of saying, "This is the body of Christ," as I have been taught to do, I practice saying, if only to myself, "This is my body broken for you." And I take the poured out wine and give it to my neighbor saying, "This is the new covenant in my blood shed for the remission of your sins."

5 Therefore, My Brothers, My Sisters

Now the Lord said to Abram, "Go from your
country and your kindred and your father's
house to the land that I will show you."
Gen. 12:1 RSV

Ever since the Church of the Saviour community came into existence more than twenty-five years ago, it has been changing and evolving. Each new stage of growth has demanded more of us, raised harder questions, and tested us at deeper levels than the one that went before. More than seven years have gone by since the fateful year of 1968 when rioting in our streets tore veils from our eyes, and let us see in searing ways some of the misery of the oppressed. At that time we struggled with our lifestyle and the disciplines that would help us to be a more radically committed people. We were laying the foundations for Jubilee Housing and other new missions, as well as deepening and expanding the ministries of existing groups.

I write this in the spring of 1976. The year of remission of sins has come again, and we find ourselves engaged in the living of a new Easter. Each day puts before our eyes sights to disturb our sleep and inform our days, and as Paulo Friere says, "Conscientization demands an Easter."

The people of Jubilee have been invited into still another building—a battered three-story structure, surrounded by equally distressed buildings. No one seems to have cared enough for this building to give it a name. Designed and licensed as a six-unit apartment house, it was long years ago divided into twelve small apartments. The lines of division went through the bathrooms. New bathrooms were never added, thus each two units share one bathroom. At times this has put an incredible strain on life in community. The tenants in one apartment sometimes

85

express their anger and frustration by refusing to share the facility with the tenants in the other, nailing the bathroom door shut. Jack Lunsford, a lawyer and member of Jubilee told us that the "unlucky ones must wash at the kitchen sink, bathe at a mission a bus-ride away and use bucket and window for toilet facilities."

Other inhabitants of the building include dogs, cats, rats, and flying, crawling things. As one ghetto dweller said of her slum dwelling, "The rats walk around in here like people." All kinds of human and animal waste are in the hallways, and trash and garbage have made the basement area uninhabitable. One's first uninformed thought is that the tenants must surely be responsible for these base conditions. Jubilee soon discovered, however, that countless efforts to secure the shattered doors had failed, and that the building is used extensively by drug addicts and derelicts in the neighborhood. The city services cannot remove the trash as quickly as it accumulates. At one of the first meetings of Jubilee with the tenants, one of their spokesmen pleaded, "If you would only send a truck around, we could shovel the stuff on."

A wooden porch fire escape is pulling away from the back of the building. A tenant says that last year an old man fell through the top floor of the porch and was killed. Despite the gross housing violations in every apartment, the tenants were afraid to complain. They knew that worse than living in a rotting apartment was living in no apartment at all. Finally the stress of intolerable conditions outweighed their fears and they began to demand that basic changes be made. The owner's response was a notice that the building had been placed on the market and the tenants would have to vacate. At a meeting with the tenants and the members of Jubilee, John Lunsford explained, "The candid rationale is that the owner wants out, by sale, if possible. But if not by sale, he would rather close the building down than to continue operating it. The cost of paying taxes with no income while waiting for the city to come along and buy it for an urban renewal program is less than operating this building as a fit, decent place of human habitation. The tenants are of no consequence to the owner." Jack, who has worked beside the oppressed since he was graduated from law school, told the tenants that they could use their anger in passive ways, or they could use it to fight for change—for a new way for themselves and for others. "If you ask us," he said, "we would like to help you in that struggle."

This fourth Jubilee building promises to play an important part in the continuing enlightenment of a people. George Davis, a member of the Jubilee Board, left the meeting with the tenants saying, "I have lived in Washington for twenty-four years and I did not know that such suffering existed. We cannot in good conscience go on living in our comfortable homes unless we are working to give everyone a decent place to live." Gordon Cosby had a similar response. "Allowing the existence of slum housing in our cities is doing violence to people. It is the equivalent of Hitler's Germany allowing the existence of the concentration camps. We cannot plead that we did not know about it." Every Jubilee member, profoundly shaken by the experience, became committed at a new level to the changing of the housing situation in Washington, underlining once again the importance of actual exposure to suffering for the education of the heart. We had all seen pictures of similar buildings and read the articles that go with them, but it was a quite different experience to be in the midst of beautiful people struggling for a worthwhile existence against unbelievable odds.

While some of our members were touring deteriorating apartments and visiting desperate tenants, Karl Menninger was touring our District jail and expressing horror not only at the physical problems of the jail—the noise, the stench, the filth and overcrowding, but the subhuman program. "There is no surprise, no break in the monotony. . . . The days go on," he said. His suggestion was that people should lock themselves in the bathroom for one day and have their meals shoved under the door to get an approximation of what prison living is like.

Conditions are equally outrageous at the District's facilities for the mentally retarded. A survey has cited that institution for failure to provide proper food, and something more than custodial care. A suit also charges that some residents have been "beaten or physically abused by the staff," and that others have been "beaten or abused either physically or sexually, by their peers."

A friend and I have struggled to put out of our minds—as though that were something necessary to accomplish—four old ladies we visited on the third floor of a dilapidated house close to the Potter's House. A poignant memory that intrudes on my life is of one old woman who kept raising her arm to shield her eyes from the glare of light coming through the uncurtained, unshaded window. I wonder how long it will be before I forget that arm so pitifully raised.

The sights are not so distressing for groups touring facilities for other helpless beings in the area of the nation's capital. In nearby Arlington a new $300,000 animal shelter has been opened. The shelter includes a sound system that pipes soothing music through the building, and a heating and air-conditioning system that completely changes the air four times an hour. Designed to house up to forty-five dogs and thirty cats the building has been described as a prototype for similar accommodations throughout the United States. The director referring proudly to the bright flourescent lights and yellow-flowered walls said, "It's bright and cheerful. We're trying to get away from the old concept of a 'dog pound' to the concept of an 'animal control and adoption center,' which better describes the purpose of our work." Arlington used $170,000 in federal revenue-sharing funds to pay part of the construction cost of the new shelter, and leased the land on which it stands for thirty years to the Animal Welfare League of Arlington for one dollar. The league is a private, nonprofit group whose operating budget this year is $115,000, of which the county contributes $65,000. The league also believes in experiential learning. Close to the entrance of the building is an education and conference room which seats about thirty-five persons. The league plans to invite school and church groups to the shelter to instruct them on such topics as the danger of pet overpopulation and how to care for animals. "We are concerned," said the director, "with the human ethic and not just animals. We are trying to show people that animals have feelings of pain and happiness. When people realize this they are more sensitive to their fellow humans."

After a few of us had visited the apartments of Jubilee's fourth building, listened to the people living there, and been lifted out of our own narrow world by seeing their plight, we wanted the same heart–expanding experience for everyone. Alive and burning in us is the hope that we can all become builders of communities of caring.

While these inequities exist all over the world, in America they are probably more hidden and thus we are deterred from becoming involved in movements for change. Also, we have a sense of hopelessness very much like the hopelessness of the poor. Deep down we do not really believe that very much can be done about the overwhelming problems of our communities. When we hear about them, we fear for ourselves, and try to secure our own houses or store up protection for our children against possible disaster. Or perhaps we are too self-centered for any concern at all. We have what we need—a way of life that is pleasing, and one in which we feel some pride—having worked for and earned it. The fact that we have more than enough in no way frees us to give attention to those who have less than enough. And then I believe that there are vast numbers of people who have known so much rejection in their lives and lived in the midst of such impoverished persons that they have never seen, close at hand, another way. Three of the most oppressed children that I know belong to one of the wealthiest families in Washington. Wealth enables their parents to leave them in the hands of servants who, though capable and efficient, know very little about good mothering, are not called to be mother and father substitutes, nor do they even know that this task has been given to them. I wonder sometimes what will become of children of this kind of oppression who, contrasted with the children of the Ritz, seem so deprived of human warmth and bodily contact. The children of the Ritz often sleep entwined around each other, and during the day are passed from one pair of arms to the next.

A friend of mine who worked for five years in the slums of Baltimore said that she became so identified with poor people that she became extremely judgmental toward rich people. "I heard judgment," she said, "in my words and in the tone of my voice. I hated it in myself because this was not my understanding of Christ who came proclaiming peace to those 'who were far off, and peace to those who were nearby.'" Though I have not had her same kind of involvement, my own long experience with oppressive structures made me know right away what she meant. When I hear the righteous note in my own words and in the words of my friends, I feel as though I am failing to be forthright, failing to give my attention to the things that should properly concern me. Jesus said, "Why do you call me good? No one is good but God alone" (Luke 18:19 RSV). Human beings all yearn for acceptance and recognition, to be needed, to love and be loved. Anyone who does not have these basic needs met will go to great lengths to set things right for herself or himself. It matters very little if one is a top executive in a thriving corporation, a worker in a ghetto project, or one of the poor. Sin enters most easily into our lives at the places of emotional deprivation.

While we must leave the judgment to God, and not become the accusers of our brothers and sisters, we still must claim the revolutionary task of making visible the oppressive conditions under which so many suffer. When we succeed in doing this for each other, we are pressed into a new kind of decision, which can be a tearing experience.

Paulo Friere, who has been a spiritual guide for so many says:

The process of conscientization leaves no one with his arms folded. It makes some unfold their arms. It leaves others with a guilt feeling, because conscientization shows us that God wants us to act.

As I conscientize myself, I realize that my brothers who don't eat, who don't laugh, who don't sing, who don't love, who live oppressed, crushed, and despised, who are less each day are suffering all this because of some reality that is causing it. And at that point I join in the action historically by genuinely loving, by having the courage to commit myself (which is no easy thing!) or I end up with a sense of guilt because I know I am not doing what I know I should. . . . I can't live my peace without commitment to men, and my commitment to men can't exist without their liberation, and their liberation can't exist without final transformation of the structures that are

Human beings all yearn for acceptance and recognition, to be needed, to love and be loved

dehumanizing them. There is only one way for me to find peace: to work for it, shoulder to shoulder with my fellow men.[1]

When the seventh year, the year of remission, drew near in our own congregation, Gordon Cosby—founder, leader, spiritual father, and brother for the Church of the Saviour community, since its founding in 1947—made a statement to the council that was to involve us in a radically new structuring of our life. His words came at the close of a long meeting:

I have just time to raise a few questions concerning my own sense of call, which is intimately related to the whole community. I have come to the place where it is not possible to carry out responsibly what I have traditionally been doing and also to help create new structures that have to do with people at the point of oppression. Ever since I can remember I have felt this as a claim on my life. It began with Garfield Hospital. From there we went to Dayspring, the Potter's House, FLOC, Dunamis, Dag Hammarskjold College, and now Jubilee Housing. At each step the community has grown. When it averaged between 60 and 70 we went through a time of redefining our corporate life. Now we have 110 members and 40 intern members, and with it a tremendous proliferation of corporate structures—legal and otherwise. All have evolved into much more demanding structures. Many have become centers of life in themselves.

As the membership has grown and the missions have expanded the time demand on us all has increased. The questions raised with me are "What is the reasonable size? When does community become so large that it cannot operate on the basis of human dimensions? How big should administrative units be?" We must look at the issue of whether as a totality we are larger than we should be. The traditional way has been to pull in more staff. I have this question as a pastor. My guess is that Bill Branner has it in the financial area. Can we keep on stretching without affecting the quality of work to which we are called?

I do not feel that it is right for me to withdraw energy from new structures that we are just beginning to develop. Have I a right to withdraw energy from these to pastor the whole, and do any of us have this right? Or can we discover ways together to move into the future without losing our richness or diversity? Is it possible that we can divide into different combinations cohering around different worship centers and, in the process of creating the new, not lose that which we value? There are many, many people in the life of this community with rare gifts of leadership that are not being used. Is it possible that we can have the Church of the Saviour at Massachusetts Avenue with its council, worship, and mission groups cohering around it; another on Columbia Road, cohering around the Potter's House; another around Dayspring?

Or is that not the way to go? Should some leave and just go out while the main body remains intact? I think we have to raise all these questions—bring them into full consciousness. Otherwise, we grow larger and larger and struggle to hold it all together, and what happens happens by default.

I am sensing an inability to be faithful to my call and also faithful to the structures that we now have. I see it as a developmental thing that every institution goes through. It can be exciting, if we do not decide to hang on—if we can look at it together. It will be difficult because there is the difficult question, "What is my place in it?" But we can work with it, struggle with it, and trust that the same Spirit which brought us to this point will still be around. We as an organization have been blessed, and my guess is that leadership might be developed at an even deeper level than we have known it.

I am not saying that I have any time schedule, or that I have a master plan, and know how to do it. I am saying that if we ask for the Holy Spirit, pray about it and talk about it, we may discover what is next for us, and that it could be a tremendously exciting and helpful time in our life.

The brief statement was to alter the life of the Church of the Saviour as had no other event in its history. There was no time for discussion at that council meeting, but in the days that followed our conversation centered around "splitting up," and "dividing." Though we strove for a more positive expression of the issues we were confronting, these words were often injected into the conversation and best described what many of us were feeling. If some felt a kind of terrible and hidden threat, others were excited about the proposal and found it full of exciting possibilities. A few bold ones began to respond to the challenge by wondering about themselves in places of leadership. While some imaginatively tried out new roles, others grew angry; still others, depressed, gave the matter no attention at all as though it would go away if properly ignored. One of our activists said, "Why don't we just do our grief work and get on with it?" The reply was that grief has its stages, and denial and anger are in its cycle.

Were size and complexity the bases of our problems, or might they be merely contributing factors? Some felt that, as the groups had developed an autonomous life, we had failed to be in dialogue with each other, failed to wait for one another, failed to keep our covenant of prayer. They argued that repentance should precede a change in structures. Mixed with feelings of joy and adventure were feelings of betrayal and hurt. In the early days of our deliberations a few even felt that they had given their lives to build a community the nature of which they had not fully understood. Family of faith, unlimited liability, brothers and sisters, life together, bearing one another's burdens, the unity of the Body, one part not held in more esteem than the other—these were all concepts that had nurtured and sustained our lives and given to us a sense of safety that had issued in creativity, love of change, and zest for risk taking. Those qualities had flourished in us, enabling us to embrace all kinds of holy insecurity. Having believed in the permanency of a particular community, we found it dreadfully painful to learn that this community was without a permanent home—literally a people in search of a city that was to come (Heb. 13:14 NEB).

One father recounted the response of his children. His son complained, "Why haven't you asked the children? We talked about it in my mission group and we don't want to change." His little girl's question was, "Daddy, who will get Gordon?"

The struggle of the children reflected that of older, wiser souls. Perhaps because this new Exodus awakened old fears of abandonment, we were not as sure that the call to build a world of justice and caring should be taken with so much seriousness. It was one thing to talk about these things and quite another to Passover ourselves from one way of life to another.

Freud had said woe to the person who tries to replace the charismatic leader. What about this leader of ours who was trying to replace or displace himself? How did we deal with all the wild clamorings that had been set in motion within and around us? What did we, who were no longer children, do with feelings of dependency that lingered on, the need and quest for a spiritual father and mother that every soul harbors. Night and day there had walked in our midst a man who had no limits around his giving, whose outpouring of life and spirit had energized our own lives and illuminated ordinary events. Who would do this for us now? Could we do it for ourselves? Or would we give up our own missions and calls and set off for the ghetto after the loved leader, or could we tap some inner strength to choose our own way, claim our own very different paths? How much of the courage and faith that we thought was ours really belonged to him?

We did not always know when we were defending what should be held onto, deepened and extended, or when we were falling into the sin of wanting to perpetuate an institution that, unlike the structures of the world, could not be concerned about enduring, but only about dying, death, and rebirth. We dreaded being "among those who shrink back and are lost," but we were uncertain that we were among those who "have the faith to make life our own" (Heb. 10:39 NEB). What did it mean at this stage of our corporate life to be a pilgrim people? Merton speaks about the journey of faith from the security of what is known to the insecurity of what is unknown. We recalled how Abraham was led out from a place he called home, where normalcy prevailed and structures could be counted on to give stability, to a place that was known surely only in the words of Yahweh. Gradually dark clouds moved away, we began to talk less about what had been, and to look with hope to the future. We spoke more about small liberating communities that would be less encumbered by problems of maintenance, and where large amounts of time usually given to maintaining the unity and healthy functioning of a large organism could flow into the building of small communities of caring, in which people could easily find a place, grow and stretch, and be given a new name. Ever so slowly we began to speak of the New Land to which our Lord was calling us, and to learn once more to name Abraham as the father of our faith.

Eight of our members were chosen by the community and "sent out" to explore the New Land. They were asked to report back to the council on what its shape might be and how the new Exodus might be made. The meetings of that group, called the New Land's Servant Group, were long and arduous. Some knew from the beginning where they were headed and how to go. They did not hide well their impatience with those who were uncertain of the Way, whose heads told them one thing and their feelings another. Among our number were also those who were process oriented, and their way clashed with those who operated in a highly intuitive way. Some wanted more prayer and less talk; others, more talk and less prayer. A few wanted to name all the alternatives and to try each on for size, so that we could find out which felt best. Some were much too literal for fantasy trips of the kind that pictured the church in diaspora—the scattered fellowship. This option included selling all the properties of the church, letting the staff go, and centering our entire focus on building small groups such as our own mission groups. The purpose would be to form communities of the people of God which would come out from the whole of society and culture in which we live, and form the nuclei of the new society. Like the Assisi community begun by St. Francis, we would endeavor to be a source of light and hope and to live in faithfulness to God's call, with values and a style of life and community which would bear witness to a society of the gospel's power. We would not only give up church property, we would share our personal material wealth with the oppressed. We would do so because of a confidence that therein lay the path of our own peace and our own experiencing of the community toward which we were journeying. We could show forth in our life together a way of human fulfillment and true liberation that might become a model for the world to insure survival for all humankind in the decades ahead. Those of us who lived our way deeply into this option saw the growth of such communities throughout the country—even the world—each committed to a common discipline and the encouragement and support of each other. Once a year, or once every seven years, we would meet together for a time of common sharing that would last for seven days. Like a special "order," the number of such groups would increase.

Such a fantasy was too threatening for some of us to live with for too long. We put it aside, knowing in our hearts that whatever the way we chose as a community, issues had been raised that would have to be dealt with in the future.

Any small group is in some way our whole world in microcosm. In the small group we recreate the experiences and relationships that we have in other combinations of persons. The Jungian analyst, Eleanor Bertine, wrote, "A new world order looms in the dense mists, and the great world-struggle is carried on in miniature within the narrow frame of a little group."[2] To the small group we each bring the hopes, fears, wishes, conflicts, projections, and expectations that move all the time in each of our beings. Those elected by the council to the New Land's Servant Group found this painfully true. We had to struggle for unity. Sometimes courageously and sometimes because we could not prevent it, we let our clay feet stick out for everyone to see. In the marriage ceremony Gordon Cosby will often say to the new wife and husband, "I charge each of you to grow to that place where each derives major satisfaction from giving satisfaction to the other." This is a charge that the church might well make to the members of each new group that forms.

After months of meeting, The New Land's Servant Group was sent on a two-day retreat. At Dayspring, amid the surroundings which had so often opened our lives and hearts at new levels to God's word for our individual pilgrimage, we began to sense together beckonings for our corporate way to the New Land.

Our retreat at Dayspring* began on Sunday evening with a communion supper. Every group session was followed by several hours of silence in which to reflect on what had been said, to listen to God's word and direction. All the meetings were in silence except for readings from devotional classics. Every new meeting began first with a sharing of feelings, and then reflections, insights and hints of the New Land. Moving within this structure our fears receded. We began to see together and in concert with each other the creative possibilities inherent in small sister communities. We began to let go of familiar ways and familiar landscapes, to take up once again the never predictable journey of a tent-dwelling people.

Wes Michaelson, who had been the scribe of all of our meetings penned the report which was presented at the next meeting of the council. In part it read:

*Retreat center of the Church of the Saviour

Our call must be our starting point. That call is to be a community centered in resolute faithfulness to Jesus Christ. It is to be his new community—those who are his body, molded by his Spirit. To build such a community of faith is our abiding call and revolutionary action.

That call encompasses the marks which our community has discovered through its history to be true and essential to its identity as God's people: the corporate commitments of spiritual discipline, the nurture of mission groups as primary crucibles of community, inner healing, growth and transformations of our lives into our true maturity in Christ, and the sacrificial outpouring of our life together in mission to the brokenness of the world.

We believe that our call as a community has four directions: First, to Christ's church throughout the world; we are part of the ecumenical church, and want to give ourselves to its life. Second, to the stranger in our midst; we are called to bring Christ's love to all those whose lives intersect at any point with ours. Third, to the poor and oppressed of this world. Fourth, to the building of our own common life; all else must flow from our call to be God's people, celebrating and nurturing ourselves as Christ's Body.

The Servant Group for the New Land repeatedly focused on three elements which describe our community's current situation: the size and complexity of our present corporate structures, the overburdening of our pastoral leadership, and the lack of full faithfulness to our covenant.

On our retreat, we further expressed our view of the issues before the community: multiplicity of demands resulting in confusion, dissipation of energy, and erosion of the sense of community.

Our task, then, is to discover structures which will better enable us to live out our corporate call. These structures should provide us with a sense of clarity, new and focused energy for outward mission and inward growth and a deeper sense of Christian community.

We believe that those structures can best be created by the formation of sister communities, each of which will function as a separate congregation, comprised of various clusters of the twenty-two existing mission groups in the Church of The Saviour. These congregations would be bound by deep spiritual ties because of their common parentage, but would be legally and organizationally independent. They would be separate churches, closely linked by history, ongoing fellowship, and potentially interlinking missions.

All mission groups, and thus the entire church membership, would probably find their lives lived out in the context of one of these communities.

The New Land's Servant Group would recommend then, that the existing Church of the Saviour be reconstituted into at least three or more sister communities of faith, with separate leadership, council, budget, organization, worship, and membership.

Such an action would restore clarity to our structures and purposes of corporate life, would enable new energies and creativity to be released for the work of the Kingdom and the deepening of our life in Christ, and the context for us all to experience and build deeper Christian community. The bonds of spiritual kinship and cooperative mission which would be nurtured between these sister communities could, and we hope would be extended toward other communities of Christ's people all over the country and all over the world.

The Church of the Saviour has been born, nurtured, and brought into fullness through the ministry of Gordon Cosby. Naturally his relationship to its future is a matter of primary concern. Through his sharing with us, Gordon has made clear that he continues to be called to the whole community, and that he would continue, if desired by any of the sister communities, to encourage the nurture of new leadership within them, and to assist in ministering on behalf of the growth of each whole. We confirm Gordon in this call.

It is our conviction that these directions will enable us to live out more fully our call to be faithful members of Christ's Body.

During the period of the meetings of the New Land's Servant Group our community used a common lectionary made up of those Scriptures that we felt would be helpful to us in our search. We titled it, *Readings for Pilgrimage to the New Land.* To the best of our abilities we had allowed our "thoughts and purposes" to be sifted by the Word of God. Alternating with long stretches of unfaith when we worried about ourselves and where we were going were other times when we touched the glory of being among those who have a vision for the earth. In those moments we were deeply aware of the unchanging love of the living Christ. Some even heard him say,

> I will never leave or forsake you. Structures will change and forms will pass away. That is how life is. I designed it that way for your sake, so that you might grow and know the peace and the lowliness and the majesty of being ultimately dependent on me.

In the days that followed the report to the council, many of us felt a new kind of solitariness. We were not lonely in any usual sense of that word. We had never had so many meetings, engaged in so many conversations, or had so little time "to ourselves." But in the midst of it we sometimes fell silent. In the long pauses we searched faces to discover kindred souls with whom we might share painful feelings of aloneness. In the end we even drew apart from the faithful friend to become Kierkegaard's "solitary individual," the one who stands alone before God, and comes face to face with his or her own "eternal responsibility." It is one thing to struggle for the corporate form of one's group or community, and another to become the solitary one who struggles for one's own destiny and vocation. Only that person who confronts each day the everlasting responsibility of being an individual can become a true builder of community.

Members of our congregation began to sound calls for the formation of new sister communities or faith communities as we sometimes called them. Everyone listened attentively to discern whether in any of these calls he was being addressed by an inner Voice.

One community is forming around Jubilee Housing, another around The Potter's House. A group is emerging to minister to those who carry political responsibility and to work with persons at the point of their vocations. A small band of people with ecological concerns is forming in rural Maryland. An emphasis of this community will be on living in harmony with nature as well as with one another. Nine adults and four children have made the down payment on a seven-unit apartment house in the inner city. At the outset this group, which calls itself The Eighth Day Community, will focus its talents and energy on being truly polycultural. The group believes that the capturing of the Christian church in the United States by the American culture should be one of the most serious concerns of Christendom, and that a new faith community truly open to the insight and inherited wisdom of all the world's cultures constitutes an authentic new vision. Another group calling itself The Seekers Community is initially gathering around worship services that will include children. This community is encouraging members to continue with existing missions until such time as new missions might emerge for them.

As some are issuing calls, others, with a kind of fervent waiting on God, are struggling to know where their places are to be. No one is left sitting on the sidelines. Everyone is engaged in a passionate way. All of us are looking at our present missions with a critical absorption, trying to envision structures and forms for the years ahead. In this quest we search for the themes that have run through our lives, knowing that if we can discover where our energies have mainly flowed, where we have felt most alive, we may discover hints of where our God is calling us, as well as integrate the future with the past.

More and more of our number are beginning to know that, despite changes in organization and geography, we will forever have the love of one another. As one member said from the beginning, "I just figure we love each other too much for it not to work out. The changes which are upon us because of God's willing and leading have the power only to strengthen the bonds we have in Christ."

As we take the risk of choosing, take the risk of new commitments, take the risk of acting, we begin to know a new sense of freedom. We are even beginning to believe that we may belong more deeply to each other, and thus be more available for dialogue with our brothers and sisters across the world.

6 Marks of the Liberating Communit

> But to all who did receive him, to those who
> have yielded him their allegiance, he gave the
> right to become children of God, not born of
> any human stock, or by the fleshly desire of a
> human father, but the offspring of God
> himself.
>
> John 1:12–13 NEB

Scripture states that "Abraham journeyed by stages" (Gen. 20:1 NEB). As our people form small communities and "set out" on the next stage of their journeying, we have pondered what might be the marks of the liberating community—the new community that will be a clear sign of God's people in the world.

First among those marks is a clear, radical, unequivocal commitment to the poorest, the weakest, and the most abused members of the human family. Among them are the children of the world whose young bodies and minds and hearts lack nourishment and protection, and who are thus condemned for the whole of their lives; the mentally ill, sprawled in the hallways of state and federal hospitals, and their brothers and sisters in misery—the mentally retarded; men and women in the prison system and juveniles in correctional institutions; the elderly on welfare; the unemployed; and those vast numbers all over the world who toil the whole day and earn barely enough to survive—to keep body and soul together. They are the neglected and despised ones with whom our Lord was so identified that he said,

> For when I was hungry you gave me nothing to eat, when thirsty nothing to drink; when I was a stranger you gave me no home, when naked you did not clothe me; when I was ill and in prison you did not come to my help. (Matt. 25:42–44 NEB)

To bear the new community's mark of commitment to the oppressed does not mean that the members will have to abandon their present callings, or betray their special gifts. What it does mean is that callings and gifts will be used for transforming the world. If I am a writer and my consciousness has been raised so that I belong not to one community, but to many communities, then what I write about and how I write about it will be different than if I never felt my unity with the whole, or sensed my place in humankind's evolutionary movement. If I am a leader of retreats, I will help my retreatants to see not only the Christ who wipes away our tears, but also the Christ who waits outside the city gate where the garbage is dumped and nothing is familiar or respectable. If I am a legislator, I will look at the laws of the land and ask not how they serve a small segment of America, but how they can serve all lands and America's revolutionary call to freedom and justice and equality. If I am a voter, I will be conscious of my responsibility to elect to office those who have a deep, abiding commitment to the oppressed. If I am a mother, I will raise children with informed hearts, as well as informed minds, not leaving to chance the development of empathy and compassion in them. If I am a teacher, the advanced students in my classroom will be encouraged to stop their own work to give slower students help in "catching up." If I am a real-estate developer, I will guard my land in such a way that the poor and the rich can live on it together. All of this may sound utopian, but the new community will bear the mark of this kind of vision. The new people of God will need to be practical. They will need a deep awareness of sin and the knowledge of how easily it mars the fairest of visions. The people of the new community will, therefore, build into their lives structures of accountability so that they can find strength and encouragement for what they aim to be and to do.

In one way, having everyone working to transform the earth is not as utopian as it sounds, because so many new possibilities open up when this way is embraced. Old attitudes slip away. There may be the same deep human need for self-esteem, but the bases for enhancement of the self are not the same. Once we took pride in how much we had: now we take pride in lowering our levels of consumption, providing health clinics, making friends of strangers, having time and energy for others, enjoying the accents of foreign tongues, and the odors of foreign foods cooking.

To the monks of Gethsemane, Thomas Merton said, "Each one of us has an irrevocable vocation to be Christ, and the Christ that I am supposed to be is irreplaceable. It has to be my vision of Christ and, if I do not fulfill that, there is going to be something missing forever and forever in the Kingdom of Heaven, and each one of us knows this and feels this."[1] What Merton says rings true in the deeps of me. I believe that the wretchedness of so many middle-class and upper-class Americans is that they are missing out on this eternal vocation. And yet this vocation to be Christ is very hard to communicate even in the churches. In the world it is rarely understood or mentioned. At the time of Dag Hammerskjöld's death I remember pausing over a news item in which a reporter stated that the United Nations leader had left a journal indicating that he was developing a messianic complex. The reporter reflected that his death might be a merciful event. He was probably referring to the book that was to be published under the title, *Markings*.[2] Perhaps Christianity can no longer be communicated except by a community which can be seen and touched. On the other hand, this has probably been the case from the beginning. Christianity has never been the sum total of its teachings, but an incarnate life. If we can be builders of liberating communities, if Christ can be lifted up, all men will be drawn to him.

The *second mark of the liberating community is commitment to a life of dialogue.* None of us will be able to make a home for the heart unless we desire with all our beings to be persons in dialogue.

In our own community we have hurt each other most when we rushed by one another without taking time either to share ourselves or to listen. We were always able to explain our failure away—at least in our own eyes—by saying that "we have too many groups for us to stay in communication;" "nothing gets done, if we all have to participate;" "these conversations drag on and on;" "we can't talk while people are shivering in the cold." These statements will have a familiar ring to anyone who is living in community where there is wide diversity of mind and temperament. They are antidialogue statements, but they are hard to confront because they are full of truth; we find them in our own hearts and on our own lips at times when we are longing to move on and the group seems to be covering the same ground over and over again, or resisting the making of a decision.

Groups are often paralyzed and fail to move in any constructive way because of the few members who want to hammer through every detail in advance, to know exactly what the future will be, to map out every step and to be certain that everyone is equally committed to picking up the pieces and bearing the costs in the eventuality of failure. In such a case commitment to dialogue does not mean that those who are positive, willing to take risks and embrace an unknown future, must always be asked to wait until everyone arrives at the same place. That will never happen. At the same time, the fearless ones cannot forge ahead as though justice and righteousness were forever on their side. If they do, they will only appear to be getting things done. In actuality they will be building structures all new on the outside and full of rotting bones inside.

When important issues have to be decided, to insure true dialogue communities and groups must learn to conduct that dialogue within the context of a passionate waiting on God. This does not mean merely beginning meetings with a time of silence, but allowing a period of silence after each one speaks so that there is opportunity to reflect on what has been said. If this seems too burdensome a way for some, then I would suggest that discussion at least be interspersed with periods of silence, so that a deeper level may be attained from which to speak and to listen.

Dialogue demands of each participant that we try to live into the other's world, try to see things as another sees them. We do not enter into dialogue in order to persuade another to see things our way. We enter into dialogue because we are open to change and are aware that our lives need correcting. Dialogue requires a clear, radical, and arduous commitment to listening. Essential to that listening is knowing in the deepest recesses of our being that we really know very little about most things, and that the truth may rest with some unlikely soul. God says to the most gifted among us, "For my thoughts are not your thoughts, and your ways are not my ways" (Isa. 55:8 NEB). When we know that, when we are truly seeking God's will we have to be persons of dialogue. The person of dialogue knows that no matter how mean, or hurt, or angry a person may be, he has something important to contribute to the dialogue. Each person in the recesses of his heart knows this about himself. He wants to speak his word and when he is not allowed to do that he feels in his being that a violence has been done to him. True listening requires that we not only listen to words, but also pay heed to feelings and acts.

The practice of listening must begin in our own households. Unless we are able to hear those in our own living and work communities, we will not be able to hear those from strange households whose ways are less known to us and who will, therefore, seem more hostile to our interests. The real test of Christian community will be not that we have warm feelings for those within our group, but whether our warmth extends to those outside the group—to the stranger, the alien. "The decisive test of brotherhood," wrote Maurice Friedman, "is not within the community, but at the boundary between community and community, people and people, church and church, for this is the place where diversity of kind and mind is felt most strongly."[3]

True dialogue is difficult for everyone. They listen well who know they have been listened to, but few of us feel really heard. I think that I can let the other go when I believe that he has truly heard my story, or point of view, or opinion. If I think he hasn't heard me, I am apt to hold him with my "glittering eye," and tell my tale over and over. The ache caused by the inability to communicate can become a kind of throbbing pain that finds expression in too many words or conversely in the silence that locks oneself in and others out, or, even more unacceptably, in the outrageous deed. In New York a group of graffiti painters made nighttime forays into a subway tunnel where they painted entire trains with garish designs. When a spark from one of the trains ignited the twenty-five cans of paint that had been stolen to complete "a piece" the boy leader, severely burned, told a reporter from his hospital bed:

> We thought we were so great. I really thought of it as an art form—the first art form born in the slums. What all of us were saying was, "Look at me, I'm somebody." Did you ever notice how people in the ghetto keep their radios by the windows playing loud into the street? It's the same thing. They're proclaiming themselves.[4]

The words of that young artist caused me to hear in a new way the noisy clamoring voices of children in the halls of the Ritz, and to look with a new awareness at the unemployed youth and men congregating on the sidewalks. What must happen to us so that we can become persons in dialogue with them? Anilo Dolci, priest and poet, working in the ghettos of Sicily wrote:

> People pass by, they pass by the millions
> Ever dense, ever more the same,
> Allowing themselves to be robbed
>   of their own lives,
> Not knowing who to cry to, and how to cry out
> "I too exist."

The third mark of the liberating community is a radical commitment to a critical contemplation of one's own life and the life of one's faith community. This commitment is important for all groups and especially important for communities like my own which have made small beginnings in aligning themselves with the oppressed, and are somewhere concretely involved in the struggle for justice. We can too easily become identified with goodness—feel that we are "the enlightened ones." We cease to ask questions about what we are doing, how we are doing it, and whether it might better be done another way. Not only must we question ourselves; we must create the kind of atmosphere that invites others to question us and to give us feedback on how they perceive and hear and experience us.

We all flower in the company of those who confirm and accept us, but sometimes the way to deeper relatedness and increased consciousness is along a more painful path. We each have characteristics and ways of responding that hurt our relationships with others—that make dialogue and community difficult—but we have no deep understanding of these failings. We have been given very little help and practice in the creative giving and receiving of feedback. We have not faced in any decisive way the fact that others have information about us that we do not have about ourselves, and that our blindness might be healed if we had the courage or ego strength to ask for it. Until we have become experienced in the giving and receiving of constructive criticism it will remain extraordinarily difficult work. I remember the friend who first instructed me in feedback techniques. After a planning session was over she put her instruction into practice and asked for our criticism, which we eagerly gave. She radiated in response to our positive feelings, but when we offered a few negative ones, she crumpled in the chair before our eyes, her radiance transformed into gloom. Afterwards we were able to laugh about that experience, but it remained a vivid lesson pointing up how fragile we all are. It is difficult enough to give helpful criticism when a person asks for it, and probably utter folly to offer it if that person is not asking. And so we stockpile negative feelings, or give our appraisal to everyone but the person in question.

What is true for the individual is also true for a community, which is apt to be even more defensive and less able to question its way of doing things and responding. The small groups of my own community have disciplines of prayer, study, worship, and tithing. To these we sometimes add other disciplines that we feel are essential for the accomplishment of our mission. It is very easy for us to think that the reason why people do not join with us is because they resist the disciplines, or that we have chosen too arduous a mission, when the real reason might be that we are a group which radiates too little joy, or seems to have all the answers, or one that will not tolerate too much questioning of its life, or any of a score of reasons.

Groups must be critical contemplatives of their corporate lives. This is the only way of protecting the dissenter, the one who sometimes turns out to be the prophet, and is too often ignored or stoned. The lonely dissenter has very little opportunity of being heard unless the group is committed to a self-questioning stance. Once a group has arrived at a course of action, defined a goal, or vested itself in a given way, its members are no longer as open to new information. Groups are even slower than individuals to change, admit mistakes, or embody humility. Having the company and comfort of one another, persons in a group, when they are questioned or asked to give an accounting, are not disturbed in the same way that a lone individual may be. A dissenter within the group learns early that any sense of belonging and community is dependent on being able to accept the stand, values, or direction of the group. If she holds to her feelings and ideas, she is apt to feel alone, outnumbered, and isolated from the warm circle of those who are sharing responses, reactions, and thoughts. To be sure, the dissenter has the option of withdrawing from the group, but then she would no longer have a community. Loss of the love that we need is too large a threat for most of us. Not without reason the dissenter fears that the aggression of group members will be used against her. The vulnerability of the one who is alone may make her more open to self-questioning, more prone to adopt what the group is saying even at the expense of her own once cherished views and thoughts. Thrown into doubt she begins to accept the arguments and opinions of the group, believing she is the only one who feels the way she does. Sometimes the words of members are harsher and more inflexible in the context of the group than they would have been had each of them met outside the group and exchanged thoughts. Again, however, gentler members, eager to assure one another that they all mean the same thing, will say, "We are just using different words—it is all a matter of semantics."

When the Christian group considers itself on mission to the world, sees itself as an agent of change in the world, the security of membership in the small liberating community can give its members the strength to speak out and work for change in dehumanizing structures. The lonely worker would lack the courage oftentimes to hold out against his work community if he did not have another place of belonging where his efforts were appreciated and his lonely acts supported. The Christian community cannot be a critical contemplative of the world and support its members who work for the transforming of oppressive institutions and not, at the same time, be a critical contemplative of its own life, listening to and protecting the existence of its own dissenters. Those dissenters have much more at stake than a job; they have at stake their belonging in a community that is fundamental and basic to their spiritual life, a community whose lifeblood flows in theirs. Like Peter, they must ask, "To whom shall we go?" (John 6:68 RSV). The major responsibility for examining its life, and for mediating love and acceptance to those who dissent rests with the Christian community which is the Body of Christ, and thus committed to truth. The Christian community knows what it is to be persecuted, and to persecute. Its own history has revealed the fact that truth sometimes rests in the camp of the enemy, and sometimes in the shouts of the "madman" whom later generations may call prophet.

The fourth mark of the liberating community is its commitment to a life of reflection. I have come to doubt that there can be any radical transformation in ourselves or the oppressive structures that we seek to change unless we value and practice reflection. Without reflection dialogue is impaired. To engage either in dialogue or any critical self-questioning without a commitment to reflection is probably impossible. So closely are dialogue, critical contemplation, and reflection intertwined that it is hard to separate them in any important way.

In reflection the emotional and the intellectual become partners. Every hour of our lives we are involved in experiencing emotions, circumstances, and events, but unless we take time to reflect on them we do not gain the essential insight that gives these diverse experiences the power to change us. Everyone is hurrying from one task to the next, or from person to person, giving only a superficial kind of attention to the outer world, and almost none at all to the inner world.

Since the beginning of its existence my new Eighth Day Community has been faced with many pressing decisions. When we begin to talk simultaneously, or do not seem to be getting anywhere, someone will say, "Let's take time to reflect on what we have been saying and what others are saying. What do we want our corporate life to show forth? What are the 'bad feelings' we may be having, and what are the 'good feelings?' What are we willing to give up and what do we feel we should hold to?" After a time we speak out of the silence, each of us sharing our reflections, each having tried to listen from a place of silence.

A few times in the empty apartments at the Mozart, I have worked with a group which has agreed to combine work and contemplation. One person was appointed to call "Stop!" when it seemed appropriate, and then we would focus on what was going on inside us at that moment. Sometimes a confession was shared. "I was feeling angry, and wishing that Kathy would bring back my tools when she borrowed them."

The work parties at the Ritz and the Mozart that had the most meaning for me were those when we sat around on the floor eating our paper-bag lunches and reflecting together on the morning's work—how we felt about what we were doing, whether we were bored or frustrated or glad to be there. We asked one another different questions; what was the dominant theme in your thinking as you worked with others, or worked alone in some closet or basement hall? What would have to happen to make our work more meaningful? What is our vision for Jubilee? What was your response to the children who came in and out of the working areas? What did this child or that child say? What was the most precious thing you received as you worked? What is the basis for praise in a roach-infested kitchen? What did you say that you wish you had not said? What do you feel good about?

Too many times we worked without reflection, without trying to gain any objective perspective on our work, or any understanding of how bits of behavior were seen by other people, or being able to check out how we were experiencing the situation and how others were experiencing it. I remember one day when the tenants joined with us in clearing the trash and garbage from one building. That day was more filled with beauty for me than almost any day that I have known. Unfolding before my eyes was my own private vision of the people of the city working together to transform the city. The Kingdom, however, did not fully come on that afternoon. Here and there were pockets of hostile feeling, and there was no opportunity for checking it out, nor was there a structure for sharing exhilaration and flashes of light. A few times someone appeared to be pushing trash into the path of someone else. One person even picked up a dead rat and "jokingly" threatened to toss it into the midst of a working group. When it became too dark to work everyone went his own way. I was glad for that day's experience, but I somehow felt terribly alone. So much had happened and, at one level, it was never shared. I didn't know what the others were thinking, and they didn't know what I was thinking. In my heart I doubted that this was the best way to build a city, even though the inspectors had warned us that they were coming the next morning.

In *A Home for the Heart*, Dr. Bettelheim describes in detail the staff meetings after each work period. One young member wrote, "The ethos of the staff meeting had the effect of making it impossible for me not to examine what I was up to—both in terms of myself and in relation to the patients. I cannot write any more about it, because I feel it would be too much like a confessional."[6]

Times of reflection, structured into the whole life of the famous school are encouraged and supported. Dr. Bettelheim writes:

> Happy feelings also seemed to demand sharing. After a celebration (not necessarily one of the great events of the year, such as Thanksgiving, Halloween, Christmas, or Easter), whatever the special event may have been, most of the staff felt a need to get together and go over what the event had meant to them before each one went on his way. How had one patient reacted to the festivities, how another? What feelings did it arouse in the staff and why? How did others deal with their feelings around such a holiday? How could it be improved on next time? This could not all be settled right after the event, but a beginning could be made before the freshness of the feelings dissipated.[7]

I know that some of my best friends will respond that the church is not a hospital, and that its small groups are not therapy groups. I have turned those thoughts over in my mind many times, and I always end up asking, "But why not?" To be therapeutic means to be healing. In Greek the root word, *therapeuein,* means to serve or to take care of. How can we say that Christ makes us whole, that he heals us, without saying that his Church is a healing community, and without asking how we can be servants of that healing? Certainly reflection was central in the life and the teaching of Christ, and in Moses before him. Moses instituted the six-day work week, which was utterly unheard of before his time, because he himself had experienced the transformation that comes through reflection. This kind of introspection is safeguarded from narcissism by the demands of the mission and its commitment to work. In the very same way action is saved from activism by the commitment to reflection, and dialogue with God, and self, and others.

If I have the fervent desire to direct the reader to Dr. Bettelheim's book, I have the same fervent desire to commend the books of Paulo Friere to those who do not know him. Friere writes of dialogue and reflection with a glistening freshness that draws one along the way of dialogue with the oppressed within our own cities. For the exiled priest, action without reflection is "lost time," as contrasted with the "'new time' with its new dimensions, in which people will triumph over their human condition."[8]

In describing the oppressed of Brazil, where the efforts of the people center almost totally on survival, he wrote:

> Brazil in transition needed urgently to find rapid and sure solutions to its distressing problems—but *solutions with the people and never for them or imposed upon them.* What was needed was to go to the people and help them to enter the historical process critically. The prerequisite for this task was a form of education enabling the people to reflect on themselves, their responsibilities, and their role in the new cultural climate— indeed to reflect on their very *power* of reflection.[9]

We will not be able to encourage reflection unless we have felt its sweeping, transforming, generating energy in our own lives. We may be able to publish journals and newspapers, renovate slum apartments, even be "good reformers," but Paulo Friere warns us that unless we teach reflection we will never be among those "who will carry out radical transformations."[10]

The fifth mark of our vocation to build liberating communities is that we will structure into every day a time of solitude. This is the foremost responsibility of the Christian revolutionary. Without a protected time of daily silence we have no possibility of doing the extraordinary inward work that each of us needs to do. Moreover, we will not make any substantial or sustained commitment to the solitary life unless we ask and seek for ourselves a structure of accountability. Anything that promises so much requires a correspondingly great effort. Unless we have a community of at least one or two who will hold us accountable, we will be tempted to take up other pursuits—unable to overcome the resistances within ourselves and distractions from without. I would especially urge that young fathers and mothers come to the aid of each other. It is hard to guard one's solitude in the midst of any need, but perhaps hardest of all in the midst of the ever present demands of the very young.

And what is this work that we will do in the silence? It is certainly a continuation of the dialogue, contemplation, and reflection that we practice in the midst of community. Our corporate involvement prepares us for a more intense one when we find ourselves alone before God. Conversely, it is also true that the dialogue with Him prepares us for a deeper encounter with the Christ in our brothers and sisters and Christ in the world. The foundation of our dialogue with God is the Scriptures. We cannot reach any new land without God's words. Through Scriptures God discloses his love for us and his vision for a just, secure and caring society. God says to us of his statutes, laws and commandments:

> You shall take these words of mine to heart and keep them in mind; you shall bind them as a sign on the hand and wear them as a phylactery on the forehead. Teach them to your children, and speak them indoors and out of doors, when you lie down and when you rise. Write them up on the door-posts of your houses and on your gates. Then you will live long, you and your children, in the land which the Lord swore to your forefathers to give them, for as long as the heavens are above the earth (Deut. 11:18–21 NEB).

We cannot put these words aside even if they arouse in us the fear of Pharisaism. Jesus in speaking about the Pharisees with their "broad phylacteries" gave us still another scripture to cling to. "The greatest among you must be your servant. For whoever exalts himself will be humbled; and whoever humbles himself will be exalted" (Matt. 23:12 NEB). The Old and the New Testaments are the handbooks for God's revolution in the world, but it is a strange revolution built upon a love relationship.

Other works of silence are confession and forgiveness. In the silence we have some possibility of being penetrated by the truth and thus of gaining the humble and contrite heart. "Forgive us our trespasses as we forgive the trespasses of others." St. Augustine called this the terrible petition, and terrible it is, because it states with alarming clarity that what we so desperately need for ourselves is conditioned upon our extending it to others—not in some far-off time, but in the moment of our asking. Despite the distinctness of the command to forgive, Scripture gives very little hint of how that powerful inward act is to be accomplished. Forgiveness is not something that can be stored away and taken out and used on some appropriate occasion. It is always of the Spirit, always new, always unfamiliar. It is an act of creation, wiping out something old and putting in its place something utterly new.

Hannah Arendt wrote:

> Forgiving, in other words, is the only reaction which does not merely re-act but acts anew and unexpectedly, unconditioned by the act which provoked it and therefore freeing from its consequences both the one who forgives and the one who is forgiven.[11]

The costly nature of forgiveness is in Christ's words, "For this is my blood of the New Testament, which is shed for many for the remission of sins" (Matt. 26:28 KJV). But Christianity is not words alone. It is a life and a cross illuminating the words. Silence offers opportunity to meditate upon the words, and the life, and the cross. That cross is at the heart of the Christian community. There is still no remission of sins without the shedding of blood. When we live in community—in close relationship with one another—we hurt each other. Those who hurt us the most are not the strangers, the ones we call enemy, but the members of our intimate circle, the ones who tell us that they love us, the ones who wish us only good. Unless the cross goes up in our own heart, unless forgiveness flows back and forth within the company of the "twelve," we will not build the New Community. Forgiveness will flow more easily if we can learn to say and to mean three difficult works that very few ever speak: "I am sorry." In order to say those words we must give up our quick rush to defend what we have done or what we have said. They require us to look ever so boldly at ourselves. Christ told us to forgive as many times as forgiveness was asked, and never to nurse our anger. He also said that we were to give our brother very concrete help in forgiving us. If, in the midst of our awareness of God, someone should cross our mind who is having trouble with us, we are to put our own life at the disposal of God (leave your gift where it is before the altar Matt. 5:24 NEB), and go to the person so that in human dialogue he might be restored to peace, and the energy of his life might flow in praise.

I have often thought of this Scripture as it relates to our trespasses against the Jews, the blacks, the poor, and the oppressed, the Vietnamese. How do we repent? How do we go to our brothers and sisters and say, "I am sorry?" Again, Christianity is not words alone. It is a life and cross illuminating the words.

Those of us who wait, however, for the other to come and ask our forgiveness cannot wait overly long. Forgiveness is integral to liberation. If we cannot forgive, we are not free. If we cannot forgive, we are not liberators. No matter how grievous the wrong, we cannot point to any deed as the reason of our present plight. Making the other responsible is not to be free. I am free only when I become responsible for who I am and what I become. My forgiveness is my willingness to be held accountable for my own life. My revolutionary vocation is to lay myself open to being hurt by even those who have hurt me once before.

The command to forgive comes to us from Christ himself. "I thank him who has made me equal to the task, Christ Jesus our Lord; I thank him for judging me worthy of this trust and appointing me to his service" (1 Tim. 1:12 NEB).

Another work of silence is intercession. We are to go to God on behalf of humanity, to go to God on behalf of the city. We are to put aside our own vision for the world and to try to draw close to God's vision. We are to image people and to image cities as God images them, so that we see them as one day they will be. In the silence we may receive the prophetic word, which is always the healing word— the word that puts another in touch with the ground of her own being.

Jesus said, "Simon, Simon, take heed: Satan has been given leave to sift all of you like wheat; but for you I have prayed that your faith not fail" (Luke 22:31 NEB). We are to pray for each other in our faith communities. We know that the advertizing industry alone has been given permission to sift us like wheat. Scarcely an hour goes by without our being bombarded by a slogan meant to generate fear, "Take that trip before you are too old to enjoy it." "You don't want him to think you don't care." Even the innocuous one of "Say it with flowers" subtly undermines our struggle to say it with our clumsy words. We are called to wrestle with God for the lives of one another, so that we, too, can say, "When I was with them, I protected by the power of thy name those whom thou hast given me, and kept them safe" (John 17:12 NEB).

Those who write on intercession usually write with strength because they can include a testimony of healing from their own experiences. My theology of intercession seemingly has been shaped more by unanswered prayers for a brother who has been for almost thirty years the victim of schizophrenia. In praying for him I have followed the instructions of the saints. I have held him in the presence of Christ more times than can be counted. I have prayed for him with only positive thoughts, seeing him well and loving and responsive to life, holding to this image despite appearances. My introduction to the Church of the Saviour was also my introduction to Agnes Sanford and the faith healers. We prayed for him then in groups and in all night and day prayer vigils. But mostly I have prayed for him alone—at the beginning and the end of every day. I think that there is no communion bread that I have not taken on his behalf.

As the masters of prayer have instructed me I have searched my heart for defiance or rebellion in myself that might block God's healing, though I admit that it is difficult for me to think that another's healing and rescue from torment would be dependent on my relationship with God, or upon my learning the lessons that he had to teach—which is another reason often given for unanswered prayer. Nor can I believe that I pray for what is not in the will of God. If God could, he would wipe away every tortured thought—every unredemptive tear.

My brother's life remains wrapped in misery and I keep praying. I may not believe quite as others believe, but nonetheless I believe. In my intercessory prayer I am addressed by God. Through intercessory prayer I have begun to know an ardent belief in man as cocreator. My prayers of intercession have led me into a more radical, incarnational theology. I believe that we are heirs with Christ and can do greater works than he did. God is not going to reach out of heaven and throw open the doors of prisons, mental institutions, and nursing homes and let the inhabitants go free, but he will infuse the hearts and minds of men and women who bow their heads on behalf of the oppressed. The Scripture says that he who dwells in love dwells in God and God in him, and Meister Eckhart adds, "Suppose I am in God, then where he is I am; and if God is in me, then unless the Scriptures lie, where I am God is. It is the absolute truth, as God is God."[12]

My intercessory prayers for someone I love does not let a cloud of forgetting come between me and that person. A ward doctor once said to me, "Surely you have become used to your brother's being ill." There is something merciful about becoming accustomed to another's suffering so that it does not have a fresh feel. To intercede for another is to keep oneself acquainted with pain—to be aware even in the most joyous moments that there are other rooms in the house where others weep anguished tears. Perhaps to intercede is to become not only a woman of joy, but a woman of sorrows. To intercede is to have one's life widen out to include all those who suffer. What if the one you love goes free? Millions of others are in the bondage from which he is delivered. To intercede is to begin to ask the question of how one might be the deliverer—to respond, "Here am I."

I believe in intercession because I believe in God as Creator who, making man in his image, has called us to be cocreators. I believe in the eighth day of creation, the making of a new world, over which we can pronounce, "It is good."

The life of intercession helps to put us in touch with the indwelling Christ and, therefore, to put others in touch with him. The atmosphere around us becomes different, making possible a wondrous sequence of events—a hearing and a seeing and an evoking that are a miracle. One might then conclude that intercession is valid because it affects the one who prays, but that is a limited understanding which does not perceive the implications of a life grounded in Christ and the resultant outpouring of Spirit. A life without intercessory prayer is deprived of sustenance and growth. It is an existence far below the poverty level.

Another work of the silence is thanksgiving. I think my own life has failed to sound notes that it might because I have not given this dimension of prayer its proper place. Close to the prayer of thanksgiving is the prayer of praise. We are to give God praise for all things. Through praise his love infuses our suffering and our struggle. Praise is to be dominant in our prayer, so that it can be the dominant note in our lives. Those of us who move amidst the tragic ask how this can be possible. The answer is, give praise and you will know. Rainer Maria Rilke makes the most direct and unencumbered reply:

> Tell us, Poet, what do you do?
> I praise. But the deadly and the monstrous things, how can you hear them?
> I praise. But what is nameless, what is anonymous, how can you call upon it?
> I praise. What right have you to be true in every disguise, behind every mask?
> I praise. How is it that the calm and the violent things like star and storm know you for their own?
> Because I praise.

A more neglected work of silence is to experience and understand our aloneness. Only in recent years have I understood the importance of this work, and how essential it is to the building of community. Too often we seek the company of others because of our dread of being alone, rather than because our love draws us into relationship. Running deep in most of us is the fear that we will be "left out." We cannot bear the thought of being neglected or overlooked, let alone replaced. These are all kindred fears. Our dread of failure can be our fear of losing friends, as our drive to the top can be our hope of winning them. We want money because we want protection against abandonment. We say yes to requests, assignments, and engagements that we might say no to if we were not afraid of losing someone's good will. We fill all the hours of the day so that we can escape the experiencing of any aloneness. We fear aging because we have absorbed the message of a culture that values production more than relationships. Those who work with the dying say that the real suffering of the dying person is not fear of death, but the fear of being abandoned.

These fears are not without the element of reality. The penniless are not respected, the old have no work to do, and the dying are often deserted even by their doctors. Nonetheless, much of the fear and anxiety that we have about loneliness is our failure to allow ourselves the pain of experiencing the fact that we are alone, and never so alone as when we suffer. Neither family, nor work, nor money, nor doctors, nor anything earthly can change the fact that we are alone with our life, which can never be fully communicated, or fully known, or fully understood by another, and sometimes not even by ourselves. This is the very same fact that makes supreme sense of the covenant of marriage and, when rightly understood, keeps any relationship to the very end exciting, mysterious, and eagerly to be explored and known.

Call it existential loneliness, if you like, or whatever will help you to grasp the painful knowledge of your aloneness that will not be relegated to some back corner of your soul. In an understanding of your aloneness lies your freedom. The work of silence is to open the door and let in the knowledge of your solitary journey, and in time to make friends with it, and to let it instruct you. Unless one does this work one never becomes fully responsible. One tends to remain what Freud called the "eternal suckling," the one that must always be nourished and taken care of, locked into the precarious, unhappy state of being unnecessarily dependent, and thus beset by fears of desertion. Without some passionate awareness that we are apart from others we never discover the ground of being where the treasure lies.

To make the struggle to stand on one's own feet—to be "the solitary individual" before God—Kierkegaard's "single one"—is to experience and accept one's aloneness. Thus do we seek in Him what we need, and transfer to Him some of our dependence on others, so that we can grow in that most important of all relationships. But even this everlasting relationship turns out to be an interdependent one. Meister Eckhart sums it up in one sentence, "God can no more do without us than we can do without him, nay, even if we turned from God it would be impossible for God to turn his back on us."[13]

If we can do this hard work of solitude—face and accept the awareness that we are alone—we are in some incredible way given to ourselves. When one belongs only to God and to one's self then comes a peace that nothing in the external can touch or take away, because it is not based on any human being or anything. "My peace I give to you; not as the world gives do I give to you" (John 14:27 RSV). Nothing in death or life can separate us from what we find within ourselves (Rom. 8:38). The heart of the New Community is a relationship with Christ. To be bound to him, to be rooted in one's own being, is to be truly liberated and to walk in the world as a free person. Then one has again the human relationships that one so sorely needs, but in a new and deeper way for now the mediator between us is Christ. The hollowness in one's self has been filled and one can turn to the other in a self-giving that is not possible when one is asking from another what no human being can give, or when one's attention is frittered away in busyness or absorbed by the clamoring children of one's own household.

Finally the work of solitude is to move into that still point of silence at the center of our lives which cannot be reached until we have made our confession, forgiven the friend, dealt with our own tumultuous thoughts, and come into possession of ourselves. "When all my house at length in silence slept," wrote St. John of the Cross, and then added,

> Upon a lucky night
> In secrecy, inscrutable to sight,
> I went without discerning
> And with no other light
> Except for that which in my heart was burning.
>
> It lit and led me through
> More certain than the light of noonday clear
> To where one waited near
> Whose presence well I knew,
> There where no other presence might appear.[14]

In the deepest recesses of our minds, in the innermost ground of being is a still, still place, where no thoughts are, where no words may be spoken, where no image may be taken, where no other creature may go. In that place God waits. One arrives there by quieting all one's faculties, closing one's eyes against all sights, one's ears against all noises, and taking all the powers of one's life and focusing them inward. For our help the author of the *Cloud of Unknowing* suggests that we take one word —*Love* or *God*—and clinging only to that word, find our way into our own innermost sanctuary. When we reach that still, deep place we have only to dwell there in the silence. The deepest prayer is nothing but loving. Any work of ours is over. In the here and now of our lives God forms in us his Son. "This birth," said St. Augustine, "is always happening. But if it happens not in me, what does it profit me? What matters is that it shall happen in me."[15]

Not only is Christ born in us, we are born in Him, sons and daughters of the Living God. In the silence God takes the essence of our being and combines it with the essence of His being. We become "heirs of God and joint heirs with Christ" (Rom. 8:17 KJV). Of this second birth, Scripture says, "But to all who did receive him, to those who have yielded him their allegiance, he gave the right to become children of God, not born of any human stock, or by the fleshly desire of a human father, but the offspring of God himself (John 1:12–13 NEB).

And how do we know when the divine birth is over—when Christ is born in us, and we are born in him? Meister Eckhart says, "The birth is not over until the heart is free from care."[16]

There is one other sign that the birth is over. When we are born a son or a daughter of the Heavenly Father and take up the vocation of Christ, then we take up the role of servant in the world, "For the divine nature was his from the first; yet he did not think to snatch at equality with God, but made himself nothing, assuming the nature of a slave" (Phil. 2:6–7 NEB). To touch a quiet center is to know that the source of action and the source of contemplation is the same—Jesus Christ. Our lives become fused with the life of God and the life of each other, and together we seek the will of God, our Father, for that small segment of the earth where we are placed.

To be a liberating community—the New Community—is to touch not only an individual quiet center, but a corporate quiet center, and to drink as a people out of wells of living water. Out of us will flow an unbelievable creativity. People will begin to marvel at what they see, but that which is happening flows out of an inner life. What is seen is visible as a result of this inwardness—an inwardness that must always be protected, nurtured, and tended.

Notes

Chapter 1

1. Dietrich Bonhoeffer, *Life Together,* trans. John W. Doberstein (New York: Harper & Row, 1954), p.1

Chapter 2

1. Paulo Friere, *The Ladoc "Keyhole" Series,* #1 (Division for Latin America–USCC, Box 6060, Washington: D.C. 20005), p.10
2. Ibid. p.25
3. Paulo Friere, *Pedagogy of the Oppressed,* trans. Myra Ramos (New York: Seabury Press, 1973), p.80
4. Paulo Friere, *Education for Critical Consciousness* (New York: Seabury Press, 1973), p.123
5. Bruno Bettelheim, *A Home for the Heart* (New York: Alfred A. Knopf, 1974), p. 307

Chapter 3

1. Alfred Delp, S.J., *The Prison Meditations of Father Delp* (New York: Herder & Herder, 1963), p.91
2. Harry Guntrip, *Psychoanalytic Theory, Therapy, and the Self* (New York: Basic Books, Inc., 1971), p. 114

Chapter 4

1. Thomas Merton, *The Asian Journal* (New York: New Directions Press, 1968), p. 337
2. Bruno Bettelheim, *A Home for the Heart,* p. 186
3. Ibid. p.7
4. Elie Wiesel, *Souls on Fire* (New York: Random House, 1972), p.257
5. Sigmund Freud, *Civilization and its Discontents* (New York: W.W. Norton & Company, 1962), p.24
6. Max Schur, M.D., *Freud: Living and Dying* (New York: International University Press, 1972), p. 421
7. Sigmund Freud, *On Creativity and the Unconsciousness: Papers on the Psychology of Art, Literature, Love, Religion* (New York: Torchbooks, Harper & Row, 1958), pp. 13-14
8. Ibid.
9. Gregory Rochlin, *Man's Aggression* (New York: Dell Publishing Company, Inc., 1973), p. 128
10. Ibid. p. 141
11. Robert Coles, *Erik H. Erikson: The Growth of His Work* (Boston: Little Brown Company, 1970), p. 82
12. New York *Times,* 10(February 1976)
13. Robert Coles, *Erik H. Erikson,* p. 132
14. Ibid. p. 254
15. Daniel Williams, *The Spirit and the Forms of Love* (New York: Harper & Row, 1968), pp. 207-208

Chapter 5

1. Paulo Friere, *The Ladoc "Keyhole" Series,* #1, p.9
2. Eleanor Bertine, "The Individual and the Group," *Jung's Contribution to Our Time,* The Collected Papers of Eleanor Bertine (J.P. Putnam's Sons for C.J. Jung Foundation)

Chapter 6

1. Thomas Merton, *The Merton Tapes* (New York: Electronic Paperbacks, P.O. Box 2, Chappaqua, Copyright © 1972 by the Trustees of the Merton Legacy Trust)
2. Dag Hammarskjöld, *Markings* (New York: Alfred A. Knopf, 1964)
3. Maurice Friedman, *Martin Buber: The Life of Dialogue* (New York: Torchbooks, Harper & Row, 1960), p. 144
4. Michael T. Kaufman, "An Underground Graffitist Pleads from Hospital: Stop Spraying," The New York *Times,* 18(October 1973), p.43
6. Bruno Bettelheim, *A Home for the Heart,* p. 400
7. Ibid. p. 396
8. Paulo Friere, *Education for Critical Consciousness,* p. 122
9. Ibid. p. 16

10. Ibid. p. 164
11. Hannah Arendt, *The Human Condition* (Chicago: University of Chicago Press, 1958 edition), p. 241
12. Meister Eckhart, *Meister Eckhart,* trans. C. deB. Evans, Vol. 1 (London: John M. Watkins, 1957)
13. Ibid.
14. St. John of the Cross, *Dark Night of the Soul,* (Baltimore, Md.: Penguin Books, 1960), p. 27
15. Meister Eckhart, *Meister Eckhart,* p. 3
16. Ibid. p. 59